Goodness, God, and Evil

Bloomsbury Studies in Philosophy of Religion
Series Editor:
Stewart Goetz

Editorial Board:
Thomas Flint, Robert Koons, Alexander Pruss, Charles Taliaferro,
Roger Trigg, David Widerker, Mark Wynn

Titles in the Series

Freedom, Teleology, and Evil
by Stewart Goetz

Image in Mind: Theism, Naturalism, and the Imagination
by Charles Taliaferro and Jil Evans

Actuality, Possibility, and Worlds
by Alexander Robert Pruss

God's Final Victory: A Comparative Philosophical Case for Universalism
by John Kronen and Eric Reitan

The Rainbow of Experiences, Critical Trust, and God
by Kai-man Kwan

Thinking Through Feeling: God, Emotion and Passibility
by Anastasia Philippa Scrutton

Philosophy and the Christian Worldview: Analysis, Assessment and Development (forthcoming)
edited by David Werther and Mark D. Linville

The Moral Argument (forthcoming)
by Paul Copan and Mark D. Linville

Well-Being and Theism (forthcoming)
by William A. Lauinger

Free Will in Philosophical Theology (forthcoming)
by Kevin Timpe

Goodness, God, and Evil

David E. Alexander

BLOOMSBURY
NEW YORK · LONDON · NEW DELHI · SYDNEY

Bloomsbury Academic
An imprint of Bloomsbury Publishing Inc

1385 Broadway	50 Bedford Square
New York	London
NY 10018	WC1B 3DP
USA	UK

www.bloomsbury.com

Bloomsbury is a registered trade mark of Bloomsbury Publishing Plc

First published in 2012 by the Continuum International Publishing Group Inc
Paperback Edition first published 2013

© David E. Alexander, 2012

All rights reserved. No part of this publication may be reproduced or transmitted in any form or by any means, electronic or mechanical, including photocopying, recording, or any information storage or retrieval system, without prior permission in writing from the publishers.

No responsibility for loss caused to any individual or organization acting on or refraining from action as a result of the material in this publication can be accepted by Bloomsbury or the author.

Library of Congress Cataloging-in-Publication Data
Alexander, David E.
Goodness, God, and evil/David E. Alexander.
p. cm. – (Continuum studies in philosophy and religion)
Includes bibliographical references (p.) and index.
ISBN 978-1-4411-3855-2 (hardcover: alk. paper) – ISBN 1-4411-3855-2
(hardcover: alk. paper) 1. Good and evil. 2. Moral realism. I. Title.
BJ1401.A49 2012
170–dc23
                                                        2012002889

ISBN: HB: 978-1-4411-3855-2
        PB: 978-1-6289-2166-3

Typeset by Newgen Imaging Systems Pvt Ltd, Chennai, India
Printed and bound in the United States of America

Contents

Acknowledgments		vi
Introduction		1
Chapter 1	Contemporary Moral Realism: Problems with a Common Assumption	6
Chapter 2	Geach's Claim: Explication and Defense	31
Chapter 3	Some Metaethical Implications of the Attributive Account of "Good"	49
Chapter 4	The Function of "Good" and Good Functions	71
Chapter 5	From the Attributive Account to God	91
Notes		125
Bibliography		147
Index		153

Acknowledgments

Quite a number of people have helped me with this project, in various ways. I wish to thank Francis Beckwith, Jay Bruce, Todd Buras, Jonathan Krull, Jon Kvanvig, Sean Riley, Brendan Ritchie, and Jonathan Sands-Wise for their willingness to talk about one or more of the arguments presented in this book.

Mike Beaty, Rob Koons, Alexander Pruss, and Margaret Watkins provided me with enormous help by thinking through many of the ideas canvassed here, as well as offering me general philosophical guidance. It is hard for me to imagine better interlocutors than these. Their desire to know the truth outweighs their desire for acclaim, but they each deserve to get both. I am confident that I am a better thinker, teacher, and friend because of their influence.

I subjected my metaphysics class to a few weeks reading through some of the material which found its way into this book. My thanks to the following students for their willingness to engage that material: Ryan Austin, Jason Bleijerveld, Jameel Brenneman, Jonathan Brenneman, Evan Cline, Nick Colgrove, Kyle Garberson, Alex Hoffman, Zach Kaufman, and Chris Valleskey. Thanks especially to Alex Hoffman for creating the index.

My friend Emily Glass did a masterful job of copyediting the entire manuscript. Emily was honest with me at every stage, pointing out the good and the bad parts. Thank you for all of your hard work and for being willing to help me out on such short notice.

Tony Bryson is not only my closest friend, but also one of the best philosophers I know. He is constantly challenging me to be clearer and to defend every single step in every single argument. His demands on me make me better in all sorts of ways. I look forward to working with him on many future projects, and most of all I look forward to giving back to him what he has given to me. Thank you, Tony. You are a true friend.

My mom and dad, Charles and Ida Alexander, encouraged me throughout the process of writing this book and helped to remind me that although being able to write a book for academics is important, it is much more important to live the ideas of such books.

Finally, I thank my wife, Genevieve, and my two kids, Julian and Angel. My wife and kids really are the sort of people that are nearly impossible not to like. I love you all so much, and it is a pleasure to be able to love each of you. I thank God every day for the wonderful gifts you are. It is to each of you that I dedicate this book.

Introduction

We confront goodness all the time: good people, places, and things. And yet we do not have an account that makes sense of the varieties of goodness.[1] My goal is to develop an account of goodness that makes sense of this variety without sacrificing unity. The theory that emerges is a version of a moral realism that relies on theses in the philosophy of language and metaphysics and ties together the varieties of goodness by arguing that all goodness points to God.

Not only is moral realism the common sense view, but it also makes more sense of moral disagreement and moral progress than moral antirealism. Yet contemporary versions of moral realism face some significant objections, which call their truth into question. Even if, however, it is true that contemporary versions of moral realism are fatally flawed, it does not follow that all versions of moral realism are fatally flawed. If we are to maintain that moral progress and moral disagreement are possible and that contemporary versions of moral realism are in trouble, then we need to develop an alternative account of moral realism that is left unscathed by the objections to these other versions.

The overall strategy I employ in this book is, first, to motivate the need for an alternative version of moral realism by critiquing contemporary versions. In the first chapter, I detail some of the problems that contemporary versions of moral realism face—problems that have not been presented in the literature. One of the problems I note and try to draw out has to do with the assumption that goodness, if it exists, is a property of some sort. More specifically, the assumption often is that goodness is a property that can figure in a posteriori necessities. I focus on the accounts provided by Richard Boyd and Robert Adams. Thus, the first chapter deals with well-developed versions—both naturalistic and supernaturalistic—of the assumption I aim to question.

I subsequently show that we need not abandon moral realism. We can abandon the assumption of most contemporary versions of moral realism that goodness is a property without thereby giving up the intuitions that motivate moral realism. In the second chapter, I begin to develop a positive account of the nature of goodness that draws heavily on Geach's account in "Good and Evil."[2]

According to Geach, the terms "good" and "bad" are logically attributive adjectives. A number of moral philosophers, working within a virtue framework (broadly conceived), appeal to an attributive account of "good" to motivate various theses. For example, Rosalind Hursthouse begins her defense of ethical naturalism by noting ". . . that 'good', like 'small', is an attributive adjective."[3] Philippa Foot begins her most recent book by claiming that the attributive account of "good" ". . . is very important and takes us some of the way in the task of bringing words back 'from their metaphysical to their everyday use'. . . ."[4] Unfortunately, neither Hursthouse nor Foot defend the main argument for an attributive account of "good" against a number of recent attacks. I remedy this deficiency by arguing that the attributive account is as plausible as any other semantics for "good." I attempt to respond to the most pressing objections as well as clear away what I take to be the most serious misunderstandings. I also address objections to my account in the third and fourth chapters but, since I think the objections and the responses to them require more setup and metaphysical heavy-lifting, I do not include them in the second chapter.

Geach goes on to argue that the semantics of "good" is incompatible with various metaethical positions (e.g. Moore's objectivism and Hare's prescriptivism). I expand upon Geach's positive claim—that "good" is essentially attributive—and his negative claim—that various metaethical positions are in conflict with the correct semantics of "good"—in an attempt to articulate a version of moral realism, which I call "Teleological Moral Realism" (TMR), which is consistent with the semantic data. I then argue that investigation into the semantics of "good," together with correlative theses regarding the metaphysics of function, reveals that the goodness of a thing depends on its nature or function.

The main idea that emerges out of the second chapter is that "good" logically requires some sort of noun to modify. The remaining three chapters (3–5) go on to argue that there are metaphysical corollaries to that linguistic doctrine that have far-reaching metaethical and even religious implications.

In the third chapter, I begin to investigate some of the metaethical implications of the Geachian account explained and defended in the second chapter. The two metaethical implications discussed are: (a) there can be no a posteriori account of the nature of goodness and (b) the goodness of a thing is based on its nature and/or function. Since the latter implication relies on the notion of function and faces apparent counterexamples, I devote another chapter to developing a metaphysics of function.

Showing that the goodness of a thing depends on its nature and function is no small task, in the fourth chapter I argue that etiological and statistical accounts of function are false and that Robert Koons's normative account is the best explanation of the metaphysics of function. Koons's view is explicitly Aristotelian and as such it is an obvious partner with the metaethical account of goodness offered in Chapter 2 and developed in Chapter 3. While Koons's approach is not free of problems, I attempt to respond to the most pressing ones and then go on to extend his account in such a way that helps the metaethical story I am telling. By the time we reach the end of Chapter 4, it should be clear that the metaethical account offered here is worth serious consideration and represents an important departure from much of the mainstream metaethical positions promulgated in the twentieth century.

One of the most obvious objections to the account of goodness I provide is based on evolutionary theory. According to this objection, by relying on natures, TMR renders/makes itself incompatible with our best theories in biological science. Evolutionary theory, we are told, was the last nail in the Aristotelian coffin. Yet, a number of contemporary biologists and philosophers of biology recognize that functions are indispensable to biology.[5] Thus, TMR's appeal to functions is not per se incompatible with evolutionary theory. Rather, its TMR's appeal to natures, such as human nature, that may seem incompatible with evolutionary theory.

We can state the evolution objection as follows. TMR assumes something like Aristotelian essentialism. Aristotelian essentialism is incompatible with evolutionary theory. Hence, TMR is false.

In response, I think that the objection may be guilty of assuming that natural selection can account for every feature of an organism. Natural selection works by selecting for traits advantageous to survival and reproduction. But evolutionary theory does not claim that natural selection produces traits. As David J. Buller notes, "[N]atural selection causes only changes in gene frequencies and, hence, changes in the frequencies of traits in a population; selection is not a cause of the presence of any trait."[6] Natural selection selects for traits already present in the population. Thus, the traits selected-for with respect to cheetahs are quite different than the traits selected-for with respect to roses—or even humans—because cheetahs, roses, and humans are different things.

The "because" in the last sentence may seem problematic. Saying that the traits are different because the things that have the traits are different appears to imply a commitment to natures. However, as is becoming clearer, evolutionary theory seems to presuppose just such a commitment.

According to Denis Walsh, evolutionary theory cannot explain why certain features are adaptive without assuming that there are stable natures in the world on which natural selection operates. He writes:

> Aristotelian natures play an explanatory role in evolutionary biology that neither the Ancients nor those who forged the current modern synthesis theory of evolution could have anticipated. Recent evolutionary developmental biology shows that one cannot understand how natural selection operating over a population of genes can lead to increased and diversified adaptation of organisms unless one understands the role of individual natures (essences) in the process of evolution.[7]

Thus, according to Walsh, Aristotelian natures play an indispensable role in explaining natural selection.

While defending a scholastic account of the natural law, Jean Porter argues that teleological explanations as well as Aristotelian natures are required to fully grasp what the scholastics had in mind. Thus, Porter too is interested in showing that there is no fundamental conflict between an ethics based on the scholastics and current biological science. After reviewing a number of prominent biologists Porter summarizes their findings as follows:

> We cannot fully understand the evolutionary history of any kind of creature without appealing to some considerations from the kinds of creatures with which we are dealing. And that means that at some points we must appeal to formal causes, that is to say explanations which irreducibly refer to the kind of creature that is in question.

If Walsh and Porter are correct, then not only does evolutionary theory not pose a threat to the metaphysics of TMR, current evolutionary theory vindicates it. Thus, TMR's explicit appeal to natures is not (or so it seems) incompatible with evolutionary theory.

Two other interesting consequences of the claim that "good" and "bad" are attributive are the convertibility of being and goodness and the privation theory of evil. In the final chapter I try to show that these are indeed consequences of the attributive claim, and I defend the privation theory of evil against its most pressing objection, namely, the badness of pain.

The convertibility of being and goodness and the privation theory of evil are theses that belong to both metaethics and philosophy of religion. Chapter 5 is, as I see it, the capstone of the book, arguing that the metaethical and metaphysical accounts offered in the first four chapters lead naturally to some fascinating theses within philosophy of religion. In particular, I endeavor to show that the convertibility thesis implies the existence of God, and that the privation theory of evil has a few implications for the problem of evil hitherto unnoticed either by its advocates or its detractors (at least to my knowledge).

I am sure that there are a large number of different reasons for writing a philosophy book. I am interested in three of them, the first two being (a) written because the author sees what needs to be said, and (b) written because the author sees what should not be said. I think my aims in this book are captured by both (a) and (b). At various points throughout the book, I think I see what needs to be said and I do my best to say it.

In my mind, Chapter 2 and parts of Chapter 5 represent this the best. In those chapters I attempt to respond to challenges that have been leveled against Peter Geach's main argument in "Good and Evil" and the privation theory of evil respectively. I think I see what should be said in response to those challenges, and, as far as I can tell, I say it. I have no doubt that I have missed various things, nor have I put an end to the debate; but I think that I have made a contribution and, I hope, furthered it in some way. For example, with respect to Geach's main argument, I am pretty sure that one of its most interesting consequences is that there is no such thing as the property of goodness.[8] But from the fact that the attributive account of "good" implies that there is no property of goodness it does not follow that there is no such thing as intrinsic value or disvalue.[9] I argue that the best way to understand the attributive account is by thinking of "good" as a predicate-forming functor or a property marker. That is, statements of the form "x is a good K" are to be understood as indicating the presence of relevant features that members of K should have in virtue of being Ks. Since many of the relevant features are intrinsic features of x, the notion of intrinsic value or goodness still has a place in an attributive account. Geach's argument is, thus, subtly but importantly different from Thomson's, and a few authors may have been misled by some of their similarities.

A saying, wrongly attributed to G. K. Chesterton, goes as follows: every time a man knocks on the door of a brothel he is seeking God. It suggests that even the desires that seem to be most distant from God or the Good are really attempts to satisfy us in ways only God can. The knocker may not know that God is the answer to his heart's deep desire, so he continues to knock on the wrong door, so to speak.

I think something similar can be said about the project undertaken in the book you are about to read. While the man in the saying knows what door he is knocking on, but does not know the real reasons why, I think I know why I am knocking on various doors, but I am not certain that I am knocking on the right ones. I am trying to knock on the door of truth, but I fear that I may have, at times, accidentally knocked on the door of the brothel down the street, so to speak. My main goal here is to rethink some of the metaethical and metaphysical assumptions that seem to underlie current thinking by proposing an alternative account and demonstrating some of the interesting consequences within metaethics, metaphysics, and philosophy of religion that flow from that alternative. At times, I think I have been successful and fairly clear. At other times, I think I have been successful and not as clear as I would like. At still other times, I honestly do not know how successful I have been. It is these latter times that both worry and excite me. They worry me, because I do not want to mislead. If there are any serious mistakes, it may indicate an equally serious misunderstanding on my part about just what it is I am trying to see and say. These same moments of tentativeness excite me, however, because I plan to continue knocking on whatever door presents itself. Even though I think I have put forth an interesting alternative to many of the current metaethical accounts of goodness as well as shown how that alternative relates to both metaphysics and philosophy of religion, at this stage in my thinking some of the topics canvassed are still coming into focus for me. I am grateful to have been given the opportunity to express them, nonetheless, and I hope to discuss them further with readers.

Chapter 1

Contemporary Moral Realism: Problems with a Common Assumption

Contemporary versions of moral realism assume that the term "good" refers to a property that falls within the scope of Kripkean and Putnamian developments in philosophy of language and metaphysics (hereafter I will use the less cumbersome KP developments). Put briefly, KP developments refer to a cluster of theses on the anti-descriptivist side of the meaning and referring divide. These theses include the claim that it is possible for certain terms—most notably proper names—to refer without descriptive content. Thus, the notion of a rigid designator—a term that refers to the same thing in every circumstance—is introduced, and the term "good" is viewed by many as being a plausible candidate for being a rigid designator. Various metaethical theories within the moral realism camp were then developed that took advantage of these insights. But these versions of moral realism face challenges strong enough to warrant an investigation into an alternative account of moral realism.

In order to defend these claims, I first explain the account of moral realism common to contemporary moral realists. Contemporary accounts of moral realism have developed in large part as a response to G. E. Moore's Open Question Argument (OQA). The OQA assumes that goodness is a property. Thus, moral realists who share this assumption must respond to the OQA by denying one of its premises. Two representative versions of moral realism, which both assume that goodness is a property that falls within the scope of KP developments and attempt to deny one of the OQA's other premises, are Richard Boyd's moral naturalism and Robert Adams's moral supernaturalism.[1] In the second section of this chapter I explain the version of naturalistic moral realism represented by Boyd. I argue that Boyd's moral realism is not plausible because of its reliance on KP styles of analysis. In the third and final section, I explain the version of supernaturalistic moral realism presented by Adams. I argue that Adams's version likely fails for reasons that he himself worries about. Thus, contemporary versions of moral realism are either in need of serious repair or should be abandoned. I will leave the repairing to their advocates. In subsequent chapters, I lay the foundations for a new version of moral realism that avoids the problems presented here.

1 Moral Realism: The Contemporary Account

In this section I argue that standard formulations of moral realism assume that "good" refers to a property susceptible to KP developments. More generally, standard forms of moral realism imply that if statements of the form "x is good" are true, goodness must be a property, that is, at least capable of figuring into synthetic a posteriori identity statements. With this purpose in mind, I limit my discussion of moral realism to two recent accounts.

In his introduction to the *Oxford Handbook of Ethical Theory*, David Copp argues that moral realism consists of the following five doctrines: "(1) There are moral properties (and relations).... (2) Some moral properties are instantiated.... (3) Moral predicates are used to ascribe moral properties.... (4) [M]oral assertions express moral beliefs.... (5) The moral properties, in that they are properties, have the metaphysical status that any other property has, whatever that status is."[2]

Copp's account of moral realism includes metaphysical and semantic claims. The metaphysical part of the account states that moral properties are on a par with other non-moral properties and that some things have moral properties. In a footnote Copp writes, "... [T]he first realist doctrine is to be interpreted such that the term 'property,' as it occurs there, ascribes the same metaphysical status to moral properties, such as *wrongness*, as it ascribes to a non-moral property such as *redness* when it is predicated of such a property."[3] Note that Copp's account is perfectly compatible with versions of moral realism that take the property *goodness* to be identical to some other property, where the identity is either analytic or synthetic.[4]

The semantic component of Copp's account of moral realism is comprised by points (3) and (4). With the assumption that moral beliefs are truth-apt, point (4) commits the Coppian moral realist to cognitivism. Cognitivism does not entail moral realism—in Copp's sense—but moral realism—again in Copp's sense—does entail cognitivism.

Copp's account of moral realism implies that moral realists must countenance moral properties and that moral properties are no different, in terms of their metaphysical status, than non-moral properties. Since, there are non-moral properties that are susceptible to KP developments, Copp leaves it open that moral properties may be susceptible to such developments as well. Copp aims to provide a general account of the commitments of moral realism, and thus leaves room for moral realists to take advantage of the semantic and metaphysical developments introduced by Kripke and Putnam. Whatever its merits or demerits, Copp's account is evidence in favor of my claim that contemporary versions of moral realism build in a commitment to moral properties that are capable of receiving a KP analysis.

Geoffrey Sayre-McCord gives a different definition of moral realism:

> Moral realists hold that there are moral facts, that it is in light of these facts that peoples' moral judgments are true or false, and that the facts being what they are (and so the judgments being true, when they are) is not merely a reflection of our thinking the facts are one way or another. That is, moral facts are what they are even when we see them incorrectly or not at all.[5]

Sayre-McCord's characterization differs from Copp's in some crucial respects. For our purposes, the most important difference is that Sayre-McCord's account does not mention moral properties. The omission of moral properties from his account suggests that one could be a moral realist and deny the existence of moral properties (but not moral facts). Nevertheless, appearances are misleading.

Sayre-McCord explains moral facts in terms of moral properties. He provides two accounts of moral facts. According to the first, ". . . moral thought and talk [is] committed to properties, and facts, and truths, that could just as well be expressed in nonmoral terms".[6] The first account goes further and claims that moral properties are identical with either natural or supernatural properties depending on who is articulating the view. The identity between moral properties and non-moral ones is thought to be knowable through analysis of moral concepts. Moore's OQA challenged the idea that an analysis of moral concepts reveals an identity between moral properties and non-moral ones. Thus, assuming Moore is right, if moral properties are identical to non-moral ones, mere analysis of moral concepts is not sufficient to reveal the identity.

Sayre-McCord's second account of moral realism is an attempt to bypass the OQA by showing that moral properties can be identical with non-moral ones even though the identity cannot be known via conceptual analysis. This account of moral realism relies on Saul Kripke's pioneering work in 1972.[7] Kripke introduced a new way of discovering property identities. Most assumed that the only way to discover property identities was via conceptual analysis. Thus, a claim that properties F and G are identical was, if true, thought to be both necessary and analytic. Kripke argued that many property identities are not knowable a priori and hence not knowable via conceptual analysis. This new wave in philosophy of language and metaphysics opened the door for a new response to Moore's OQA. Moral properties could be identical with non-moral properties without there having to be synonymy between the moral predicate and the non-moral predicate that refer to these properties. In Sayre-McCord's view:

> But the most powerful grounds for rejecting the Open Question Argument came with the realization that two terms, say "water" and "H_2O," could refer to one and the same property, even though one would be asking a substantive question (that can be settled only by investigating the world) in asking whether H_2O is

water. The realization that a proposed identity could both be true and yet fail the test of the Open Question Argument encouraged the hope that, after all, a naturalized metaphysics for moral properties could be defended.[8]

Despite the fact that Sayre-McCord's characterization of moral realism does not mention moral properties, it is clear from his exposition that moral facts include moral properties. Indeed, as is clear from the above quotation, Sayre-McCord's account of moral realism explicitly includes reference to moral properties that are capable of KP analysis.

Standard accounts of moral realism include, either explicitly or implicitly, reference to moral properties that are capable of figuring in analytic or synthetic property identities. In particular, most moral realists are committed to the claim that goodness is a property that is either analytically or synthetically identical to some other property. Consequently, the moral anti-realist need only show that each project fails in order to establish her/his position.[9] If the anti-realist can show that moral properties are neither analytically equivalent to non-moral properties, nor synthetically equivalent to non-moral properties, then moral realism is false, given the assumption that these are the only two options.

The chief aim of this book is to argue that the standard account of moral realism implicitly assumes a false dichotomy (or trichotomy if we insert moral non-naturalism back into the list of options for moral realists). There is another option for moral realists besides the analytic and synthetic ones currently offered. Before providing the details of this third option, however, it is important to see some of the shortcomings of the analytic and synthetic accounts.

2 From Moore's OQA to A Posteriori Moral Naturalism

In order to be a moral realist one must be a naturalist, non-naturalist, or a supernaturalist. If G. E. Moore is correct, moral naturalism is a non-starter. Moore's OQA aimed to show that no naturalistic definition of a moral term is possible. Here is a reconstruction of Moore's main argument: Either goodness is simple or goodness is complex.[10] If goodness is complex, then analysis should reveal its constituents. But analysis does not reveal the constituents of goodness. Hence, goodness is not complex. The OQA is Moore's defense of the minor premise. Any identification of the property goodness with some other property (i.e. goodness = F) will always leave it an open question whether the other property is indeed good. But since property identifications are a matter of analysis, and if goodness is in fact identical with F, the question "is F good?" should never be open. Since it is open, there is no property that goodness is identical with, and hence goodness is not complex. Since analytic moral naturalism and analytic moral supernaturalism, which claim that the definition of "good" is both analytic and purely descriptive, appeared to be the only options for the moral naturalist and supernaturalist, these versions of moral realism looked doomed. Hence, if one opts for moral realism, and the OQA is sound, then one must be a non-naturalist. But non-naturalism falls prey to a host of objections that have convinced most that non-naturalistic moral realism is plainly false.[11] Hence, given the soundness of the OQA, moral realism is false.

Through the work of Saul Kripke and Hilary Putnam, a plausible semantics for synthetic property identities was developed.[12] Moral naturalists and supernaturalists attempted to appropriate this work in order to show that the nature of goodness is entirely natural or supernatural but cannot be known a priori. Hence, it is possible, according to their theory, to provide a definition of "good" that is purely descriptive but *not* analytic. If this appropriation is successful, a version of moral naturalism emerges that avoids the OQA. To date, Richard Boyd's "How to be a Moral Realist" is the most discussed account of a semantics for "good" that attempts to show that like "tiger," "water," and other natural kind terms, "good" may refer to a property or kind that can be synthetically identified with a natural property.[13] In the next section I present a novel argument that Boyd's account fails.[14]

2.1 Moore's OQA, Boyd's Response, and Trouble

The motivation behind moral realists' turn toward the work of Kripke and Putnam comes primarily from G. E. Moore's OQA. By allegedly showing that neither moral naturalism nor moral supernaturalism is correct, Moore's commitment to moral realism forced him to embrace a version of moral non-naturalism. But Moore's conclusion that goodness is simple, unanalyzable, and knowable only through intuition has left most moral realists unsatisfied.[15]

In the early 1970's Kripke and Putnam put forth a new semantics that explained how synthetic property identities are possible. Kripke and Putnam supported their semantics by arguing against the then prevalent descriptivism. One of the assumptions of descriptivism is that necessary truths and a priori truths are co-extensive. The identity of water and H_2O appears to show that it is possible for at least some statements—that is, water is H_2O—to be necessarily true but not knowable a priori. This advance opened the way for those moral realists not willing to embrace non-naturalism to respond to the OQA.

If synthetic property identities are possible with respect to natural kinds and if "good" is a natural kind term (or something like one), it may be that the proposition expressed by "good = F" is necessary but not knowable a priori. Thus, the OQA is unsound, since one of its assumptions—that property identifications are a matter of analysis—is false. Richard Boyd's semantics for "good" argues just that. According to Boyd:

> The reference of a term is established by causal connections of the right sort between the use of the term and (instances of) its referent.... *Roughly*, and for nondegenerate cases, a term *t* refers to a kind (property, relation, etc.) *k* just in case there exist causal mechanisms whose tendency is to bring it about, over time, that what is predicated of the term *t* will be approximately true of *k* (excuse the blurring of the use-mention distinction). Such mechanisms will typically include the existence of procedures which are approximately accurate for recognizing members or instances of *k* (at least for easy cases) and which relevantly govern the use of *t*, the social transmission of certain relevantly approximately true beliefs regarding *k*, formulated as claims about *t* (again excuse the slight to the use-mention distinction), a pattern of deference to experts on *k* with respect to the use of *t*, etc. When relations of this sort obtain, we may think of the properties of *k* as regulating the use of *t* (via such causal relations), and we may think of what is said using *t* as providing us with socially coordinated *epistemic access* to *k*; *t* refers to *k* (in nondegenerate cases) just in case the socially coordinated use of *t* provides significant epistemic access to *k*, and not to other kinds (properties, etc.).[16]

Boyd's semantic account for moral terms attempts to establish that moral terms, like natural kind terms, are rigid designators and are thus subject to the causal theory of reference (CTR). A term *t* is a rigid designator just in case *t* refers to the same thing in every possible world.[17] If, for example, "good" is not a rigid designator, then "good" refers to different properties at different times or in different possible worlds; "good" would not refer to a kind that causally regulates the use of "good." The resulting theory would be a form of moral relativism not compatible with moral realism.

Rigidity and CTR are also needed to explain how two different terms can refer to the same thing despite the fact that it is not possible to know that the terms refer to the same thing without empirical investigation. The OQA is thus blocked for terms that are both rigid and subject to CTR. CTR claims that reference can be grounded through an initial "baptism" or "dubbing" ceremony where the referent is baptized with some general or singular term. Subsequent uses of the term—reference-borrowing—are made possible by a causal chain leading from current uses back to the original baptism. For example, our use of "tiger" refers to all and only tigers, in part, because of some initial labeling of a tiger or group of tigers with the term "tiger." Furthermore, the initial baptism of tigers as "tiger" need not have had any true descriptive content. According to Kripke, "we might ... find out tigers had none of the properties by which we originally identified them."[18] The descriptions we use to fix the reference of some term are all contingently true at best. Boyd's semantic account appears to be committed to the following theses:

> *Causal semantic naturalism* (CSN): Each moral term *t* rigidly designates the natural property *N* that uniquely causally regulates the use of *t* by humans.[19]

Pure Causal Theory of Reference (PCTR): Reference-grounding is determined by way of an initial baptism such that it is possible that the initial baptism of some natural kind *K* or individual *I* with term *t* have entirely false descriptive content; and reference-borrowing is determined by way of an appropriate causal/historical chain leading from present uses of *t* to the initial baptism of *K* or *I* with *t*.

The trouble for Boyd's account is not difficult to see.[20] In order to avoid the force of the OQA, Boyd (like others who wish to appeal to synthetic property identities) has to appeal to the possibility that "good" refers to some natural property *N*, without the descriptive content of "good" uniquely determining a referent. If the descriptive content of "good" uniquely determines a referent, then the nature of the referent will be known a priori and it will be possible to run the OQA. This suggests that Boyd would accept PCTR. From these commitments we can construct the following argument against Boyd's account:

1. If *t* is a kind term susceptible to PCTR, then the nature of the referent of *t* is only discoverable empirically.
2. If the nature of the referent of *t* is only discoverable empirically, then it is possible for the nature of the referent of *t* to have the same extension as the referent of some other kind term that falls within the scope of PCTR.
3. Hence, if *t* is a kind term susceptible to PCTR, then it is possible for the nature of the referent of *t* to have the same extension as the referent of some other kind term that falls within the scope of PCTR.

Assume that "good" is a kind term that falls within the scope of PCTR. The nature of goodness is thus only discoverable empirically. Given (2), it is possible that the nature of goodness is the same as the nature of badness or rightness or pleasantness or . . . (assuming, as seems perfectly permissible, that if "good" is a kind term susceptible to PCTR then the others may be as well). But it is absurd to suppose that the nature of goodness could be the same as the nature of badness. It may not be absurd on some theories of morality to identify the nature of goodness with the nature of rightness or pleasantness, but according to other theories such identities are absurd. The point is that once we allow that "good" is a kind term that can be understood according to PCTR, the theorizing involved in moral philosophy is a waste of time.[21]

This objection assumes a pure version of CTR. PCTR has recently come under scrutiny. Many philosophers now reject PCTR, replacing it with a hybrid theory of reference according to which true descriptions must be a part of reference-grounding.[22] In the next section I present the hybrid theory and a revised version of Boyd's semantic account. I argue that the revised version also fails as a semantic account for moral terms.

2.2 The Hybrid Theory and The Moral Qua-Problem

According to the pure causal theory of reference, singular terms and some general terms are capable of referring without either the reference-grounder or reference-borrower having any correct descriptive content in mind. PCTR is implausible not only with respect to moral terms but with respect to non-moral terms as well. For any naming ceremony, the referent is a member of numerous kinds (natural and non-natural). If the term is supposed to pick out the species (in the case of natural kind terms) or the individual (in the case of proper names) and nothing else, then reference-grounding must include at least some correct descriptive content. If reference-grounding does not include any correct descriptive content, then the term could refer to any of the numerous kinds of which the referent is a member. For example, S comes into contact with members of some species. S baptizes these members as "tigers." According to PCTR, S's initial baptism refers to all and only tigers. But S's initial confrontation with tigers was also a confrontation with cats, mammals, animals, time slices of tigers, individual tigers, etc. How is it that S's baptism of the members of the kind tigers with "tiger" is a baptism of all and only tigers and not cats, or mammals, or animals, or etc.? The fact that members of natural kinds belong to an infinite number of kinds—natural or gerrymandered—suggests that PCTR is, as it stands, incomplete. Nothing in PCTR seems to rule out the possibility that S's initial baptism was a baptism of a different kind or even a disjunction of more than one kind.

This objection to PCTR is now called the qua-problem. We need an account of reference-grounding for "tiger" that gets the extension of the term right. That is, we need an account of S's initial baptism that explains how S managed to refer to tigers qua tigers and not tigers qua cat, or qua mammal, or etc.

The most common answer to the qua-problem is a hybrid theory where PCTR is replaced with something like the following:

> *Hybrid Causal Theory of Reference* (HCTR): Reference-grounding is determined by way of an initial baptism, but it is not possible that the initial baptism of some natural kind K or individual I with term t have entirely false descriptive content—the initial baptizer(s) of K or I with t must have some correct description of K or I in mind; and reference-borrowing is determined by way of an appropriate causal/historical chain leading from present uses of t to the initial baptism of K or I with t.

The only difference between HCTR and PCTR is that the hybrid account states that the initial baptizer must have some correct descriptive content in mind. HCTR appears to be capable of handling the qua-problem for singular and natural kind terms.

S refers to tigers qua tigers and not qua cats because S has some correct description of the members of the species that are before her that picks out tigers but not cats or animals or mammals, etc. It is a matter of some dispute what description S must have in mind when baptizing members of the tiger species.[23] For our purposes, what is important is not the exact nature of the description but rather that some kind of description is needed.

The fact that PCTR assumes that baptizers can have completely false descriptive content in mind when baptizing gave rise to some potentially absurd consequences for Boyd's semantic account. HCTR blocks those consequences. We can amend Boyd's account:

> *Causal semantic naturalism* (CSN*): Each moral term *t* rigidly designates the natural property N that uniquely causally regulates the use of *t* by humans, and when N is baptized *t* by S, S must have in mind some correct description of N.

The additional clause will block some of the absurd consequences, but it will not solve all of the problems.

It is important to keep in mind that Boyd's semantic account is a response to the OQA, and like nearly every moral naturalistic account it assumes that the prospects for defending analytic moral naturalism are bleak. Consequently, the descriptive content that S has in mind when baptizing N with "good" had better not fall prey to the OQA. In other words, when S baptizes N with "good," the description D that S has in mind must be such that all N things (i.e. all good things) are D. But the converse must not hold. If the converse—all things that satisfy D are N (i.e. good)—held as well, then the resulting biconditional—D iff N—would rule out the possibility of a synthetic property identity. The OQA enters straightforwardly at this point. The most that the baptizer can hope for then is that all instances of the thing baptized are members of the D class (i.e. the class of things that satisfy the description). If it turns out that some things that are clearly N are not in the D class, then it will be possible to run a slightly weaker version of the OQA. For example, if S baptizes the thing before her with "tiger" and S has in mind the description "quadruped," then it should turn out that every tiger is a member of the quadruped class. Whatever fails to satisfy the description is not a tiger. The fact that there are tigers that are not quadrupeds shows that the description was incorrect. According to HCTR, S must baptize with a correct description in mind. Thus, if we can legitimately wonder whether all the things that fall under the baptizing term satisfy the description, we have good evidence that the description will not work to secure reference.

The situation is even more difficult when it comes to specifying the correct description used by S when baptizing a natural property with a moral term. If the descriptive content that S has in mind is *philosophically* contentious, the purported identity between "good" and N cannot be established until the philosophical debates reach a conclusion. Suppose, for example, that S baptizes N as good with the description ". . . results in pleasure" in mind. It should follow that every subsequent use of "good"—cases of reference-borrowing—also satisfies this description, just as every subsequent use of "tiger" should satisfy the description ". . . is a species." But, of course, there is widespread disagreement about whether uses of "good" must always satisfy the description ". . . results in pleasure." A philosophically controversial description used during the reference-grounding and carried into reference-borrowing threatens to result in a misunderstanding of the nature of the referent. Those who do not think that "good" always falls under the description ". . . results in pleasure" will not accept any subsequent empirical investigation into the nature of goodness that relies on the description ". . . results in pleasure." Thus, before the a posteriori identity between goodness and N is established, the philosophical debates regarding the descriptions used to pick out goodness (and thus secure reference) need to be settled. Indeed, the descriptions used in the naming ceremony must be both a priori and platitudinous.[24] Trouble is lurking nearby.

Remember that for any naming ceremony, the referent is a member of numerous kinds (natural and non-natural). Take the purported referent of "good." Whatever the purported referent of "good," that referent will be a member of numerous kinds. To see this, simply take any determinate and consider its determinable or take any species and consider its kind, and so on.[25] In order to get the reference relation right and avoid the qua-problem, the initial baptizer must have had some correct descriptive content in mind. But what descriptive content could the initial baptizer have had in mind that avoids the OQA by being both a priori and not philosophically contentious?

One suggestion might be that the descriptive content S had in mind when baptizing N with "good" was simply ". . . is an action." Does ". . . is an action" pass the above tests? No. It is false that all things that are good are actions (or at the very least it is philosophically contentious that all things that are good are actions). Furthermore, actions fall under various other kinds, and it is implausible to think that all good things will also fall under these other kinds. For example, actions are happenings, events, non-substantial, etc. Is it at all plausible to think that all good things are happenings, events, non-substantial, etc.?[26] The OQA is applicable to each of these. For just about any descriptive content we imagine the initial baptizer to have in mind the problem is that descriptive content falls prey to our new version of the OQA and is thus philosophically contentious.

There may be a way out of the above problem. Instead of looking for some descriptive content that the initial baptizer had in mind, which secures reference to goodness and only goodness, perhaps we should consider the possibility that there are conceptual constraints on our use of "good." For example, the supervenience of the moral on the non-moral and the action-guidingness of the moral may be conceptually necessary truths that constrain our use of "good." Flout these in your use of "good" and you are not a competent user of the term.[27]

It is important to see exactly what this response concedes. There are a priori truths—indeed analytic truths—about the nature of goodness. In other words, the response slides us much closer to descriptivism than those who are committed to an account of the nature of goodness in terms of synthetic property identities may be willing to allow. Furthermore, it may be that careful attention to our a priori knowledge of what goodness is will result in determining the referent of "good." If this possibility is open, then while a posteriori knowledge may help in securing reference, it will not be needed. If a posteriori knowledge is not needed, then we do not have a synthetic property identity. So, granting that we have some a priori knowledge of the nature of goodness threatens the entire project of avoiding the OQA by claiming that the nature of goodness cannot be known a priori.

Perhaps my objections against the a posteriori moral naturalist are not decisive. Simply conceding that we must have some a priori knowledge of the nature of goodness does not imply that the entire nature of goodness is knowable a priori. After all it does not follow from the fact that since we must know at least part of the natures of tigers, water, and gold a priori (given HCTR) that it is possible to know the complete natures of tigers, water, and gold a priori.

In general, the inference from "S knows part of the nature of K a priori" to "it is possible that S knows all of the nature of K a priori" does not follow because the natures of natural kinds are microscopic structures. Since the natures of natural kinds are microscopic structures, we know that the only way to discover them is via empirical investigation. That is, we know a priori that if the essence of K is a microscopic structure, then the essence of K cannot be known a priori. But do we have any reason to think that the essence of goodness is similar? Not only do we not have good reasons to think that the essence of goodness is similar in structure to the essence of natural kinds, we actually have good reason to suspect that the essence of goodness is not at all similar.

The multiple realizability of goodness suggests that there is not some microscopic structure that is the essence of goodness. If there were such a structure, then it is plausible to suppose that goodness could not be multiply realizable in the way that it is. But since goodness is multiply realizable, it does not have some microscopic structure that is only knowable via empirical investigation. Thus, we have good reason to believe that "good" is not a natural kind term and hence that goodness does not have a natural essence.[28]

Granting that there are conceptual constraints on our use of "good" does not help solve the above worries. The conceptual constraints must not determine the nature of the referent. Thus, it must be the case that the nature of goodness is partially known at the time of reference-grounding and that it is not possible to know the nature of goodness entirely apart from empirical investigation. But for the reasons canvassed above it is implausible to suppose that the nature of goodness is in any way like the nature of natural kinds.

We have seen that attempts to argue that "good" is like a natural kind term face serious, perhaps insurmountable problems. For the moment assume that the project is able to get off the ground. That is, assume that the conceptual constraints for "good" are all worked out and the conceptual constraints clearly do not determine the nature of the referent. Should we conclude that synthetic moral naturalism is at least partially vindicated? I do not think we should. Synthetic moral naturalism would not be vindicated because a more serious qua-problem can be raised.

In order to see the more serious qua-problem, consider that every *morally* good thing—every morally good person, act, institution, state of affairs, etc.—instantiates *non-moral* goodness as well. Good persons are alive, good acts are complete, good institutions are working, good states of affairs are obtaining, or possibly obtaining.[29] Every time the property of moral goodness is instantiated, the property of non-moral goodness is instantiated as well.[30] To explain this, the synthetic moral naturalist must claim that the initial baptizer had in mind moral goodness and not non-moral goodness when she baptized N with "good." If she did not, then the moral qua problem looms. But what exactly is the difference, and is it at all realistic to think that initial baptizers had the difference in mind?

Perhaps the difference between moral goodness and non-moral goodness is that the former is concerned with persons while the latter is not. But persons instantiate non-moral goodness. To repeat: for any instance of *moral* goodness, an instance of *non-moral* goodness is present. This is why the moral qua problem is much more serious than the qua problem for natural kinds.[31]

Synthetic moral naturalism does not appear to be sustainable. Moore's OQA shows us that analytic moral naturalism is implausible. If these are the only two live options for the naturalistic moral realist, naturalistic moral realism appears implausible.

However, appearances are misleading. This section (along with the one to follow) is meant to provide moral realists with the motivation to reconsider one of their most pervasive assumptions; that goodness is a property susceptible to KP analysis. Indeed, as will become clear in Chapters 2, 3, and 5, I aim to give moral realists some reasons to reconsider the assumption that goodness is a property—full stop. If it is possible to be a moral realist and deny that goodness is such a property, or even a property at all, then it is possible for there to be a version of moral realism that is left completely untouched by the above concerns. With a posteriori moral naturalism behind us we will direct our attention to a posteriori moral supernaturalism to see if it fares any better.

3 Adams's Moral Supernaturalism

Robert Adams's defense of a divine command theory of moral obligation has received quite a bit of attention. Surprisingly, his articulation and defense of a Platonic version of theistic moral realism has not received nearly as much attention. In this section I attempt to fill that void by criticizing Adams's endeavor to separate the semantics from the metaphysics of ethical terms—in particular the term "good." If I am correct, then a significant portion of Adams's ethical framework needs serious revision. Furthermore, since Adams's divine command theory relies on his axiology, the criticisms raised here indirectly put pressure on his divine command theory as well.

In *Finite and Infinite Goods* Adams seems to argue that the proposition expressed by "goodness is faithfully resembling God" is a posteriori necessary.[32] Adams defends this claim by appeal to KP developments. Adams calls moral theories that endorse the view that "goodness is faithfully resembling God" versions of theistic Platonism. Yet, upon inspection of his argument it is evident that a competent user of "good" could know that goodness is faithfully resembling God without anything like empirical investigation (i.e. a competent user of "good" could know a priori that goodness is faithfully resembling God). If the details of Adams's account are correct, then "goodness is faithfully resembling God" is a priori necessary, not a posteriori necessary. Thus, Adams's appeal to recent developments within philosophy of language fails. According to Adams, if theistic Platonism implies that the nature of goodness can be known a priori, then theistic Platonism is implausible. I will argue that Adams's own version of theistic Platonism implies that the nature of goodness can be known a priori. Hence, Adams's own version is implausible. And since his version is by far the most developed supernaturalistic a posteriori moral realism, all similar accounts likely fail as well.[33]

3.1 The Theory

Adams begins *Finite and Infinite Goods* by characterizing the nature of the Good. In connection with a Platonic conception of the Good, Adams notes that this notion "is not *usefulness*, or merely instrumental goodness. It is not *well-being*, or what is good for a person. It is rather the goodness of that which is worthy of love or admiration."[34] Adams states that he will be pursuing a version of theistic Platonism—the view that, "The role that belongs to the Form of the Good in Plato's thought is assigned to God, and the goodness of other things is understood in terms of their standing in some relation, usually conceived as a sort of resemblance, to God."[35]

In the section titled "The Semantics and the Metaphysics of Value" Adams relies on KP developments in the philosophy of language in order to dispel what once was considered an insurmountable obstacle facing a Platonistic conception of the Good. If metaethics is meaning-analysis and nothing more, then theistic Platonism is quite implausible since it is clear that the meaning of goodness is not "faithfully resembles God."[36] With the emergence of the new semantics for certain referring expressions (e.g. "water"), we can separate the meaning of a word from the nature of the thing the word signifies. Hence, although the meaning of "goodness" is not "faithfully resembling God," this now poses no threat to theistic Platonism since, in general, it is no longer thought to be the case that the meaning of some term *t* is or reveals the nature of the referent of *t*. In other words, given plausible theses in the philosophy of language, it is possible to claim that the *nature* of goodness is distinct from and not revealed in the *meaning* of goodness.

Adams spells out some of the details of the KP account as follows:

> This approach has been developed most famously with respect to natural kinds. It is the nature of water to be H_2O, it is claimed; and the property of being water is, necessarily, identical with the property of being H_2O. But the word "water" does not *mean* H_2O. What I must know, at least implicitly, about water in order to understand the sense of the word "water," and so to be a competent user of the word, is that if there is a single chemical nature shared by most of the stuff that I and other English-speakers have been calling "water," then, of necessity, all and only stuff of that nature is water. The causal relations between concrete samples of water, on the one hand, and users and uses of the word "water," on the other hand, serve to "fix the reference" of the word—that is, to determine which stuff the word names. But the nature of water is to be discovered in the water and not in our concepts.[37]

At least three important points emerge from this passage. First, in order for the claim that "necessarily, water is H_2O" to be true, the following necessary a priori claim must be true as well: "if water has a certain type of chemical nature, then necessarily that chemical nature is water." Second, the proposition expressed by "necessarily, water is H_2O" is only knowable a posteriori. This is crucial to Adams's account, since if it were knowable a priori, the nature of water would not have to be discovered *in the water*. If the nature of water could be discovered without investigating the water, then the distinction between meaning and nature collapses. The meaning of the term would reveal the nature of the referent. These two points show that Adams is sticking pretty closely to the standard argument schema for a posteriori necessities, which looks something like this:

1. If *P*, then necessarily *P*.
2. *P*.
3. Therefore, necessarily *P*.

The first premise is arrived via a priori reflection. The second premise is arrived at via empirical investigation and is therefore a posteriori. Thus, the conclusion is a posteriori necessary.

The third point Adams draws attention to is the CTR. As we have seen, according to CTR, the referent of a term is fixed by some causal connection between the referent and users of the term. So, samples of water help to fix the reference of the term "water," but the descriptions used to fix the reference do not reveal the nature of the referent.[38] Generalizing from the water example, we have the following three claims:

1. A necessary proposition knowable only a posteriori about the nature, x, of a natural kind is based on a related necessary proposition knowable a priori.
2. With respect to some natural kind terms the nature, x, of the referent is knowable only a posteriori. Hence, there are some necessary propositions knowable only a posteriori (as seen in the argument schema above)
3. The causal theory of reference explains the connection between some thing x and our use of a natural kind term for x without making it necessary that the meaning of the natural kind term includes the nature of x.

Adams claims that applying these developments in the philosophy of language to metaethics affords surprising results.

According to Adams the above account of the necessary a posteriori together with a more general account of reference-fixing than the one provided by the causal theory of reference is applicable to at least some ethical terms.

> I am proposing that we do use ethical terms in an analogous way [analogous to what the CTR says with respect to natural kind terms], which enables us to distinguish between the semantics of ethical discourse and what we may call the metaphysical part of ethical theory. Not that good, for example, is a natural kind; but the meaning of the word "good" may be related to the nature of the good in something like the way that has been proposed for natural kinds.[39]

Adams's proposal is to use the new semantics in order to separate the semantics of ethical discourse from the metaphysics of ethical theory. As noted already, doing so is necessary for the plausibility of theistic Platonism.

Adams is quick to point out disanalogies between the causal theory of reference for natural kinds and for goodness. He states, "As good is not a natural kind in the way that water is, the meaning of the word 'good' does not direct us to anything like a chemical structure. And we cannot assume that causal interactions with concrete samples will fix the reference of 'good' in the same way that the reference of 'water' is fixed."[40] Hence, Adams wants to free his theory from a commitment to (3). But now we are in need of some other story that accounts for the connection between our uses of "good" and the things that are good.

Adams attempts to fill this gap by providing a "general pattern for the relations of natures to meanings where the nature is not given by the meaning."[41] According to Adams the meanings of both natural kind terms and ethics terms indicate a role that the referent of the terms is to play. "What is given by the meanings, or perhaps more broadly by the use of the words, is a role that the nature is to play. If there is a single candidate that best fills the role, that will be the nature of the thing."[42] So instead of (3) Adams proposes something like the following:

> (3*) The best candidate theory of reference explains the connection between the nature of x—for example, goodness is faithfully resembling God—and our use of a term for x—for example, "good"—without making it necessary that the meaning of "good" includes the nature of goodness.

In the case of water, a natural kind, its nature is assigned the role of accounting causally for its observable properties. H_2O, it turns out, plays that role. With respect to goodness, Adams maintains that "faithful resemblance to God" is the best candidate to fill the roles revealed by our uses of the term "good." The task given to the ethicist is to determine the meanings of ethical terms and thus determine the role that the referent of ethical terms plays.[43] Adams does just this.

The first role, according to Adams, that is indicated by the meaning of the word "good" that the bearer of this property must play is that of being something other than a state of affairs. "A good candidate for the role of goodness in the sense of excellence . . . will not be a property of states of affairs."[44] The second role revealed by the meaning of "goodness" is that goodness is treated as a property of things, possession of which is independent of creaturely cognizers. This role implies that in at least one context of use "good" is best understood realistically. Adams recognizes that the semantics of goodness does not entail the truth of realism. His claim is simply meant to express the idea that if a candidate exists that allows for the truth of realism, then this candidate fits the semantic data better than a candidate that does not allow for the truth of realism.[45]

The next role for goodness mentioned by Adams and revealed by the meaning of "goodness," is that the Good is pursued as an object of Eros. "Eros . . . prize[s] its object as intrinsically valuable. Being, at least, an object of Eros is an important part of the role which the excellent has in our lives and which is therefore assigned to it by our language."[46] Furthermore, the Good is not only pursed as an object of Eros, the Good is also admired. Indeed, according to Adams, the pursuit of the Good ". . . arises from the admiration."[47] In response to an objection to this claim, Adams uncovers another role that is assigned to goodness by the meaning of the term. The objection is that we make mistakes about what is good in that we often pursue and admire what is not, in fact, good. Adams grants the point but notes that his theory denies that the Good is to be analyzed in terms of desire. Rather, the analysis goes the other way. Our desires are to be understood as responding to what we take to be good, and this cannot be a wholly unreliable process. "Goodness is therefore an object not only of admiration and desire, but also of *recognition*, at least commonly and to some degree."[48]

Thus far we have uncovered a number of roles revealed by the meaning of the term "good" which the referent of "good" must satisfy. Adams goes on to indicate a few others. Good things will be related to the Good in a number of ways. In particular they will not be against the Good. While being for the Good, desiring the Good, and loving the Good may be appropriate ways to understand how persons relate to the Good without being against it, being for the Good is not broad enough to include every excellence. Thus, Adams claims that "[r]esemblance to the Good is a more plausible candidate."[49]

With the above roles in mind Adams argues that the best candidate for filling the roles ". . . is a person or importantly like a person."[50] He writes:

> . . . [M]ost of the excellences that are most important to us, and of whose value we are most confident are excellences of persons or of qualities or actions or works or lives or stories of persons. So if excellence consists in resembling or imaging a being that is the Good itself, nothing is more important to the role of Good itself than that persons and their properties should be able to resemble or image it. That is obviously likelier to be possible if the Good itself is a person or importantly like a person.[51]

Adams next argues that Anselm's ontological argument may be recast as a metaethical argument showing that the Good must actually exist. Thus, the roles revealed to us by the meaning of goodness imply that the single best candidate that satisfies all of the roles is the Good itself, which is a person who actually exists.

Earlier I highlighted three claims involved in Adams's treatment of a posteriori necessities for natural kind terms. Adams's account of goodness seems to me to be problematic with respect to both theses (2) and (3*). In the next section I will raise some concerns regarding (3*), and follow those up with a section critiquing thesis (2), since that claim seems to be more central.

3.2 Adams and Thesis (3*)

> Thesis (3*) states: The best candidate theory of reference explains the connection between the nature of x and our use of a term for x without making it necessary that the meaning of "good" includes the nature of goodness.

The causal theory was presented by Kripke, Putnam, and others as a way of explaining how the reference of a term can be fixed without descriptions used to fix the reference expressing necessary truths about the referent. For example, we may fix the reference of water via various descriptions—for example, being drinkable, tasteless, odorless, etc.—without any of these descriptions revealing anything about the nature of water. It is possible that each of the descriptions we use to fix the reference of a term is false. Water need not be drinkable, tasteless, odorless, etc. in order to be water. As noted in Section 2.2, the qua problem raises serious concerns for this way of articulating the theory, but the hybrid solution appears to leave room for a causal theory without succumbing to full-blown descriptivism.

Adams does not attempt to use the causal theory of reference in order to distinguish the semantics of goodness from its metaphysics or nature. Instead, he attempts to generalize from the causal theory of reference to a theory of reference that captures what is involved in fixing the reference of natural kind terms *and* certain moral terms. It is worth quoting the relevant portion of Adams's discussion again. He writes, "What is given by the meanings, or perhaps more broadly by the use of the words, is a role that the nature is to play. If there is a single candidate that best fills the role, that will be the nature of the thing."[52] This sketch of a theory is supposed to account for both natural kind terms and moral terms.

However, Adams's theory of reference seems to suggest that he must abandon direct reference theory. That is, Adams's preferred account of reference-fixing not only replaces the causal theory but jettisons the direct reference theory as well. Robert Stalnaker states the theory that contrasts with the direct reference theory thus:

> The contrasting answer that [Kripke] argued against is that the semantic value of a name is a general concept that mediates between a name and its referent: a concept of the kind that might be expressed by a definite description. According to this contrasting answer, the semantic value of the name—its sense or connotation—determines a referent for the name as a function of the facts: the referent, if there is one, is the unique individual that fits the concept, or perhaps the individual that best fits the concept.[53]

Adams's theory of reference states that uses of a term specify roles that the referent of the term is supposed to play. Whatever (if anything) best fills these roles is the nature of the term. Thus, if any one thing best fills the roles indicated by our use of the term "good," then that thing is the nature of goodness. Similarly, if any one thing best fills the roles indicated by our use of "water," then that thing is the nature of water. Adams states this explicitly.

> ... H_2O and [XYZ] may be assumed to have analogous structures which are causally relevant in analogous ways to their shared observable properties. Why not say, then, that it is not being H_2O, but a structural property common to

H_2O and [XYZ], that accounts causally for the observed properties of water, even on planet Earth? The answer, I think, must be that the explanation of the observed properties in terms of H_2O is a *better* explanation than that in terms of the more abstract and complex structural property common to the two chemical compositions....[54]

Adams's theory of reference seems to be a best candidate theory of reference. One important point should be noted. On twin earth the best candidate to fill the roles indicated by uses of "water" does not have the property of being H_2O but rather the property of being XYZ. Thus, it seems that on Adams's account water is H_2O on earth and water is XYZ on twin earth. But then "water is H_2O" does not express an a posteriori necessary proposition. Perhaps a story will help illustrate this point. Let us assume that the descriptions we use to fix the reference of the term "water" are d, d^*, and d^{**}. Whatever (if anything) best satisfies these descriptions is the nature of water. It turns out that after empirical investigation H_2O best satisfies these descriptions. Thus H_2O is the nature of water. Now go to twin earth. On twin earth the descriptions twin earthlings use to fix the reference of the term "water" are d, d^*, and d^{**}. Whatever (if anything) best satisfies these descriptions is the nature of water. It turns out that after empirical investigation XYZ best satisfies these descriptions. Thus, XYZ is the nature of water. Both H_2O and XYZ are the nature of water.

The objection raised in this section claimed that Adams's theory of reference appears to commit him to denying that water is H_2O is a posteriori necessary. If whatever best fills the roles indicated by our uses of some term is the nature of the referent, then if two different things equally satisfy those roles, those things are the nature of the referent of the term.[55] This seems to follow straightforwardly from Adams's preferred theory of reference.

Of course, Adams anticipates this when he notes that we say that H_2O is the nature of water and not XYZ because H_2O must be the better explanation. What Adams does not tell us is why H_2O is the better explanation. I suspect that H_2O is the better explanation precisely because we are in causal contact with the kind H_2O, and not with the kind XYZ. That is, the reason, or at least part of the reason, for selecting H_2O as the nature of water and not some complex property shared by H_2O and XYZ is encapsulated in CTR. Thus, (3*) is not enough to secure the a posteriori necessity of "water is H_2O." CTR is needed. We have therefore been given no reason to replace CTR with (3*) and, if the worry expressed in this section is correct, we have been given some reason not to replace CTR with (3*).

3.3 Adams and Thesis (2)

Thesis (2) states: With respect to some natural kind terms the nature, x, of the referent is knowable only a posteriori. Hence, there are some necessary propositions knowable only a posteriori.

According to Adams one necessary proposition knowable only a posteriori is that goodness is faithfully resembling God.[56] Adams's account does not provide any indication that this proposition can *only* be known a posteriori. Indeed, his account seems to imply that the proposition expressed by "goodness is faithfully resembling God" is knowable a priori.

The roles revealed by our use of "goodness" point us toward the nature of the thing that satisfies the roles. That is, if S competently uses the term "good," then S will know, or be in a position to know, the roles indicated by her/his use of "good." But if S knows the roles indicated by goodness, it is possible for S to discover the nature of the thing satisfying these roles. Hence, a competent user of goodness will be able to discover the nature of the thing satisfying these roles. Thus, with respect to goodness the semantics reveals the metaphysics. According to Adams, "Platonist theories of the Good . . . are not very plausible as accounts of what is ordinarily *meant* by 'good'."[57] It turns out that if Adams is right about this, then his theory is not very plausible.

A defense of the above objection is in order. Why think that the roles revealed by our use of goodness determine the nature of the thing that satisfies them and, thus, that Adams's account fails to show that empirical investigation is necessary to determine the best candidate for satisfying the roles revealed by our use of goodness? Well, in one sense this question hardly needs asking. What empirical investigation could be necessary to determine the best candidate for satisfying the roles revealed by our use of goodness (assuming for the sake of argument that the roles Adams uncovers are correct) if it turns out that the best candidate is God? If we grant that the roles provided by Adams are the right ones, then it seems that God is indeed the best candidate that satisfies the roles. In the presentation of the roles revealed by the meaning of "goodness" we saw that Adams is able to arrive at the conclusion (based on inference to the best explanation) that the best candidate for satisfying the roles is an actually existing person. This is, of course, the conclusion that Adams wants. But it is not arrived at in the way Adams needs. If Adams is to keep the semantics of "good" separate from the metaphysics of goodness as excellence, then some empirical investigation must be required in order to determine the referent of the roles. Adams provides none. He states, "A theistic theory of the nature of excellence obviously presupposes or implies the existence of God."[58] What should not be obvious, for Adams's theory at least, is that an account of the meaning or roles indicated by our use of "goodness" implies the nature of the referent as a matter of conceptual analysis. Yet, according to Adams, all of the roles taken together imply just that.

That the roles revealed by the meaning of "goodness" imply the nature of the referent can be seen from the discussion earlier of Adams's more general theory of reference. After empirical investigation, the best candidate to satisfy the roles indicated by our use of "water" turns out to be H_2O. Thus, empirical investigation is needed in order to determine the nature of the referent of "water." The semantics of "water" is separate from the metaphysics of water because empirical investigation is required to discover the nature of the referent of "water." According to Adams, the best candidate that satisfies the roles indicated by our use of "goodness" turns out to be faithful resemblance to God. However, Adams does not rely on empirical investigation when he argues that "faithfully resembling God" is the best candidate to fill the appropriate roles revealed by our use of "good." Rather, the fact that "faithfully resembling God" best fills the relevant roles is discovered simply by considering what would have to be the case given the roles indicated by our use of "goodness." Notice, that this is true even if no a priori proof for God's existence is possible. If it turns out that the only way to know that God exists is to experience Him or aspects of creation, it does not follow that experience is necessary to know that the nature of goodness is faithfully resembling God. As long as we already possess the concept goodness and the concept God, then given the roles indicated by our use of goodness we can know a priori that the nature of goodness is faithfully resembling God. Nothing Adams has said, as far as I can tell, suggests otherwise. Thus, despite Adams's attempt to provide a general theory of reference that covers both natural kind terms and "goodness," the fact that the nature of the former must be discovered empirically does not in any way imply that the nature of the latter must be discovered empirically as well.

Recall that Adams appeared committed to the standard argument schema for a posteriori necessities. According to that schema:

1. If P, then necessarily P.
2. P.
3. Therefore, necessarily P.

The conclusion is a posteriori necessary because the second premise is a posteriori. Adams's attempt to show that the proposition "goodness is resembling God" is a posteriori necessary appears to follow the standard schema:

1. If goodness is resembling God, then necessarily goodness is resembling God.
2. Goodness is resembling God.
3. Therefore, necessarily goodness is resembling God.

Again, in order for the conclusion to express an a posteriori necessity it must be the case that the second premise is only knowable a posteriori. But as I have been urging Adams's proposal suggests that the second premise is knowable a priori. Hence, the conclusion is knowable a priori as well.

Two examples from Adams's text provide evidence for the claim that the connection he draws is a priori and not a posteriori. Consider Adams's discussion of Anselm's ontological argument. He suggests that the argument "may indeed be best interpreted in a metaethical context, as an argument that supreme Good must be understood as an existing being and moreover as existing necessarily."[59] This is a provocative suggestion, but it only weakens Adams's case for the claim that the nature of goodness is discovered as an a posteriori necessity in an analogous fashion that water was discovered to be H_2O.[60] The metaethical version of the ontological argument shows that the supreme Good must exist. Thus, one can know a priori not a posteriori that the supreme Good must exist. Given that a competent user of "good" will (in some sense) know the roles that must be satisfied by goodness, a competent user is in a position to know a priori both that the roles are indeed satisfied (via the metaethical ontological argument) and that goodness is resembling the supreme Good (i.e. God).

A second example is Adams's argument for the implausibility of thinking that the being that satisfies the roles of goodness is merely possible. He writes, ". . . the Good is a being that actually appreciates things and has actual aims and actual causal influence on other things."[61] The roles of appreciation, aiming, and casual influence are used here to argue a priori that the Good is an actual personal being and not simply a possible being. Not only do we not need to engage in empirical investigation to discover the nature of goodness, we also do not need to engage in empirical investigation to discover if that nature is exemplified. Competent possession of the concept of goodness reveals the roles that must be satisfied in order for goodness to have a referent. Furthermore, competent possession of the concept of goodness reveals that the nature of the referent is an actual person. Hence, competent possession of the concept of goodness reveals both the meaning of the term "good" and the nature of its referent. Indeed, competent possession of the concept of goodness reveals that the nature of goodness is exemplified. Thesis (2) is not satisfied.

The most promising line of objection to my criticism is to challenge my reading of Adams's claim that goodness is resembling God. I have suggested that the most natural reading of Adams's claim is that the relevant proposition is an instance of the a posteriori necessary. I argued that Adams has provided us with no reason to think this is so and with a number of reasons to think it is not so. But, says the objector, it is plausible to interpret Adams's claim in a different way. According to one route this objection might take, I have presented the case in such a way that the meaning of "goodness" somehow includes "resembles God." In other words, this criticism of Adams is basically that Adams gives us no reason to believe that it is a posteriori necessary that goodness is resembling God, and every reason to believe that it is analytic that goodness is resembling God (assuming for the sake of argument the details of Adams's account). But it is implausible to think that it is analytic that goodness is resembling

God. After all, Adams's work shows that it takes a great deal of philosophical ingenuity to make the case that resembling God is the nature of goodness.[62] What this objection amounts to, it seems, is that we should construe Adams's claim as a synthetic a priori proposition and not as an analytic one. I contend that this objection fails to save Adams's account.

Going the synthetic a priori route still makes the connection between goodness and resembling God a priori. Indeed, standard examples of synthetic a priori truths are of propositions that provide constraints on conceptual competency with respect to some domain of discourse. Just think of other possible candidates of the synthetic a priori—for example, that nothing can be completely red and completely blue or that every event must have a cause or that the moral supervenes on the non-moral. Assuming that these are indeed instances of the synthetic a priori it is easy also to see that they impose conceptual constraints on one's grasp of event, color, and moral concepts. That is, a competent user of event words or color words or moral words must grasp these a priori connections (at least dispositionally). If the same is true for Adams's claim that the connection between goodness and resembling God is synthetic a priori, then we should expect this instance of the synthetic a priori also to impose conceptual constraints on competent usage of goodness. But this is precisely what Adams wants to avoid. Competent users of goodness need not be in a position to know that goodness is resembling God. Hence, the synthetic a priori move does not help Adams.

There is a second route that the objection I am considering might take. Instead of granting me that the connection between the nature of goodness and resembling God can be known a priori (given the soundness of Adams's argument), one might claim that we have conflated empirical knowledge with a posteriori knowledge. The argument, it is granted, has shown that Adams's account cannot succeed as a defense of the claim that the nature of goodness is only knowable empirically. But, it is urged, my criticism has not shown that Adams's account cannot succeed as a defense of the claim that the nature of goodness in only knowable a posteriori. Now, if empirical knowledge and a posteriori knowledge are co-extensive, the argument works. But I have not provided any reason to believe they are co-extensive.

While I think this version of the objection may have some legs, I am not convinced. One reason for my ambivalence is that when pressed this objection often looks suspiciously similar to the first version canvassed above. For example, what, I may ask, is the alternative account of the a posteriori that does not conflate this with the empirical? Apart from some genuine alternative I suspect that this objection is simply another way of putting the above failed objection.

Another reason I am not moved by this second take on the objection is that I have yet to hear a plausible alternative version of the a posteriori. I grant that articulating the distinction between the a priori and the a posteriori is quite hard (I certainly do not have a novel theory to offer). Nevertheless, Adams relies on such a distinction. After all he spends quite a bit of time articulating the KP account and applying almost all of it to ethical terms. While he does reformulate one element of that account his reformulation is not meant to be incompatible with the KP account and as far as I can tell his reformulation does not force a different construal of the a posteriori. If I am wrong in thinking that Adams has not provided good reasons for believing that the nature of goodness is resembling God is an a posteriori necessity because I have conflated the a posteriori with the empirical, then I can recast our concern in the following way: While Adams's claim that it is a posteriori necessary that goodness is resembling God fails if a posteriori is taken to be closely connected to the empirical, Adams's claim may not fail if a posteriori is radically divorced from the empirical. Given the latter possibility the current objection is thus not a refutation of Adams's claim but simply a challenge (a powerful one, I think, but I am biased) to Adams to provide a plausible way to understand what kind of a posteriori knowledge he has in mind when arguing for the claim that it is a posteriori necessary that goodness is resembling God.

A different response to the objection raised in this section maintains that Adams could amend his claim that it is a posteriori necessary that goodness is faithfully resembling God. In its place he could put that it is a posteriori contingent that goodness is faithfully resembling God. If it is a posteriori contingent that goodness is faithfully resembling God, then in some other world the claim is false. The difficulty with replacing a posteriori necessity with a posteriori contingency is that it seems to have the unwelcome consequence that a world qualitatively identical to our own is such that "goodness is faithfully resembling God" is false. So why think that it is true in this world? Notice that this consequence follows even if God is a necessary being. If "goodness is faithfully resembling God" is a posteriori contingent, the relation between goodness and faithfully resembling God is contingent. Nothing follows about the modal status of the relata. Thus, if Adams makes the amendment I suggest then he would have to hold that there is a world such that God exists in it and goodness exists in it but the identity between goodness and God does not hold. But now it is a mystery as to why the identity holds in this world. Any appeal to abduction would equally apply in the other world since it is qualitatively like our own.

It is safe to conclude that Adams's attempt to identify goodness with resemblance to God either fails or is in need of revision. Given a grasp of the concept goodness and a grasp of the concept God, one can discover without any empirical investigation that goodness is some sort of resemblance to God (granting of course that Adams's account of the meaning of goodness is basically correct). Thus, Adams's attempt to appropriate recent developments in the philosophy of language fails. If the arguments presented in this section and in Section 3.2 are sound, then Adams's version of moral supernaturalism cannot save moral realism from the grip of Moore's OQA.

4 Conclusion

In their current guises, both moral naturalism and moral supernaturalism rely heavily on KP styles of analysis in order to avoid the OQA and other problems. The failures of a posteriori moral naturalism and a posteriori moral supernaturalism together with the failures of analytic moral naturalism and analytic moral supernaturalism are taken by many to signal the end of moral realism. In the following chapters, I attempt to show that there is an alternative conception of goodness that does not succumb to the objections presented in this chapter.

For those not convinced by the arguments presented in this chapter against a posteriori moral naturalism and a posteriori moral supernaturalism, I offer the following bit of consolation. In Chapters 2 and 3 I argue that the semantics and logic of "good" reveal that goodness is not a property of the sort that can figure in a posteriori necessities. Indeed, as I suggest in Chapter 5 goodness is best thought of as not being a property at all. The basis of that argument is a defense of Peter Geach's claim that "good" is an attributive adjective, and, as such, cannot stand alone. If that is right, and if the metaphysical corollary—that goodness cannot stand alone—is correct, then we have the ingredients for an indirect argument against the moral theories discussed in this chapter. Boyd's moral naturalism and Adams's moral supernaturalism implicitly assumed that "good" is not an attributive adjective. Both accounts seemed to assume that it is possible to make sense of "good" all by itself. That is, both accounts simply relied on common philosophical usage of statements of the form "x is good." For Adams the relevant notion was goodness as excellence, and the idea seemed to be that it is perfectly acceptable to think that there is such a thing as plain old excellence. For Boyd the relevant notion was simply goodness, but he too seemed to assume that we can understand goodness apart from its modifying something else. My suggestion in the next two chapters is that this cannot be right. So, if the arguments put forth in this chapter did not persuade you, my hope is that the arguments of Chapters 2 and 3 will have some pull.

CHAPTER 2

GEACH'S CLAIM: EXPLICATION AND DEFENSE

At the end of Chapter 1, I concluded that the standard ways of articulating and defending moral realism face what seem to be insurmountable obstacles. If analytic moral realism and synthetic moral realism are the only options, then moral realism is in serious trouble. In this chapter I argue that there is a third option, hitherto neglected by most moral philosophers. According to the third option, defended by P. T. Geach, "good" and "bad" are always attributive adjectives.[1] The attributive nature of "good" and "bad" reveals something important about the ontological status of their referents. Of particular interest, the attributive nature of "good" and "bad" reveals that their referents are not properties of the sort that fall within the scope of Kripke and Putnam's revolutions in philosophy of language and metaphysics.

In order to understand the claim that "good" and "bad" are always attributive, I present and elaborate on an argument given by Geach. I then go on to briefly defend Geach's claim by either refuting or neutralizing common objections. In the chapter to follow I will indicate the relevance of Geach's claim to the common assumption that goodness is a property that can figure in synthetic property identities. Indeed, as will become clear by the end of the book I will argue that it is a mistake to think that goodness is a property—full stop.

1 Geach's Argument

In "Good and Evil" Geach argues that there is a logical distinction between predicative and attributive adjectives. Predicative adjectives differ from attributive adjectives in terms of the types of inference that each allows. Consider the form "x is a(n) A N" where A is an adjective and N is a noun. If it is valid to infer that "x is an A" and "x is an N" from "x is a(n) A N," then A is predicative. For example, from "x is a red bike" it is valid to infer that "x is red" and "x is a bike." Hence, "red" is a predicative adjective.

Attributive adjectives, on the other hand are those adjectives that do not permit the above type of inference. Again, consider the form "x is a(n)

A N." If it is not valid to infer that "*x* is an *A*" and "*x* is an *N*," from "*x* is a(n) *A N*," then *A* is attributive. For example, from "*x* is a big flea" it is not valid to infer that "*x* is big" and "*x* is a flea." Hence, "big" is attributive. If such an inference were permissible it could easily be shown that "*x* is a big animal" follows from "*x* is a big flea," which of course it does not.[2] The following argument schemas illustrate these differences:

Splitting Test

Logically Predicative: *x* is a(n) *A N* ⊨ *x* is *A* and *x* is a(n) *N*.
Logically Attributive: *x* is a(n) *A N* ⊭ *x* is *A* and *x* is a(n) *N*.[3]

Thus, logically predicative adjectives pass what I will call the splitting test, while logically attributive adjectives do not.

According to Geach, "good" is an attributive adjective. Geach reasons as follows. If "good" were a predicative adjective then in the schema "*x* is a good *N*" it would be permissible to infer "*x* is good" and "*x* is an *N*" just as it is permissible to infer from "*x* is a red *N*" that "*x* is red" and "*x* is an *N*." From *x* is a red bike we may infer that *x* is a red vehicle since all bikes are vehicles. But with respect to the adjective "good" similar inferences do not follow. From "John is a good chemist" we cannot infer both that "John is good" and "John is a chemist." If we could, then it would follow from "John is a good chemist" and "All chemists are persons" that "John is a good person." Clearly this is an invalid inference.[4] Since the assumption that "good" is a predicative adjective licenses invalid inferences, we must reject the assumption. "Good" is not a predicative adjective.

"Bad" is attributive because, Geach claims, it is something like an *alienans* adjective. Since *alienans* adjectives are attributive and "bad" is like an *alienans*, bad is also attributive.[5] Examples of *alienans* adjectives are "forged," "putative," "alleged," and "artificial." The adjectives are *alienans* for at least two reasons. First, they function like attributive adjectives in that it is not valid to split the adjective and the noun. For example, it is not valid to move from "*x* is a forged banknote" to "*x* is forged" and "*x* is a banknote," since a forged banknote is not a banknote. Second, *alienans* adjectives differ from other attributive adjectives in that statements true of an *N* will not necessarily be true of an *N* plus *alienans*. Few of the true statements about horses are true of rocking horses.[6]

While it is not valid to infer that "bad" is attributive from the claims that bad is *like* an *alienans* adjective and *alienans* adjectives are attributive, Geach does enough to show that "bad" is attributive. *Alienans* adjectives have the two features spelled out in the previous paragraph—(a) it is invalid to split an *alienans* adjective from the noun it modifies and (b) what is true of the noun that the *alienans* modifies is not necessarily true of the noun plus *alienans*. These two features are sufficient for *alienans* adjectives to be in the class of attributive adjectives. Indeed, given Geach's earlier argument that the essential difference between attributive and predicative adjectives is that the latter but not the former pass the splitting test the fact that *alienans* adjectives do not pass the splitting test is sufficient for *alienans* adjectives to be in the class of attributive adjectives. Since "bad" does not pass the splitting test, it belongs to the attributive class. Geach's reference to *alienans* adjectives is beside the point.[7] Even if "bad" does not belong to the class of *alienans* adjectives, the mere fact that "bad" does not pass the splitting test is enough to ensure that "bad" is an attributive adjective.

Geach claims that these considerations show that "good" and "bad" are essentially attributive. That is, it is necessary that for all x, if x is good, then x is a good K.[8] Another way of stating Geach's thesis is that "good" is a non-intersective adjective. If we think of the meaning of a predicate as a set, then intersective adjectives are those adjectives that can combine with other intersectives such that the meaning of the combination is the intersection of the two sets. For example, in "x is a red ball" the predicate means the intersection of the set of red things with the set of things that are balls. Notice that if A and N are intersective, then it is valid to infer from "x is A N" to "x is A" and "x is N." "Good" does not appear to behave like an intersective adjective. If it did, then the meaning of the predicate in "x is a good man" would be the intersection of the set of good things with the set of things that are men. But this apparently assumes that from "x is a good man" it is valid to infer "x is good" and "x is a man," which it is not.[9]

Furthermore, notice that if x is a red K and x is also a member of some distinct kind K^*, then x is also a red K^*. For example, from "x is a red bike" and "all bikes are vehicles" we may infer that x is a red vehicle. Similarly, from "x is a red vehicle" and "x is a bike" we may infer that x is a red bike. When the noun that a predicative adjective modifies belongs either to a higher-order kind or a lower-order kind the predicative adjective modifies those kinds as well. This does not hold for good Ks. From "x is a good K" and "x is also a member of some distinct kind K^* (higher or lower-order)" it does not follow that "x is also a good K^*." When the noun that an attributive adjective modifies belongs either to a higher-order kind or a lower-order kind it is not necessarily the case that the attributive adjective modifies those kinds as well. The following argument schemas illustrate these points:

Higher-Order and Lower-Order Kind Test
Logically Predicative: x is a(n) AK and x is a(n) $K^* \vDash x$ is a(n) AK^*
Logically Attributive: x is a(n) AK and x is a(n) $K^* \nvDash x$ is a(n) AK^*

Thus, logically predicative adjectives pass what I will call the higher-order and lower-order kind test, while logically attributive adjectives do not.

2 Some Corollaries

Geach appears to think that the noun "good" modifies must denote something with a function or a nature. Geach expresses this point as follows: "If I do not know what hygrometers are for, I do not really know what 'hygrometer' means, and *therefore* do not really know what 'good hygrometer' means; I merely know that I could find out its meaning by finding out what hygrometers were for...."[10] Hence, in order to understand the phrase "good x" I must know the function or essence of whatever takes the value of x.[11] In general, for instances of the claim "x is a good K" to be intelligible, the value of K must refer to something with a function or nature.[12]

In his *The Virtues,* Geach relaxes his claim that to understand the phrase "good x" one must know the function of x.[13] Geach argues that it is possible to know all sorts of things that are good for humans without knowing the function of humans. For example, we know that a just government is good for humans and that temperance is good for humans without knowing what humans are for.

Geach's reasoning seems to be that since it is possible to know many things that are good for humans without knowing what humans are for, it is not necessary to know what humans are for in order to understand the statement "x is a good human." But this does not follow. What is needed is a premise to the effect that it is possible to understand the statement "x is a good human" without understanding what humans are for. In the next chapter I will argue that natures and functions are intimately connected. More specifically, I will argue that in some cases the nature of a thing determines its function, while in other cases the function of a thing determines its nature. Thus, in order for Geach's new argument to go through, he would have to argue that it is possible to understand the statement "x is a good human" without understanding the nature of a human. But this seems implausible. If I do not know the nature of humans, then I do not know whether justice and temperance are good for them. Surely it is conceptually possible that Thrasymachus was right and justice is actually bad for humans.

Geach does point to a feature that is important by relaxing the claim that to understand "x is a good K" we have to understand what K's are for. It is implausible to think that in order to understand "x is a good K" we must have a *comprehensive* understanding of the function or nature of Ks. A limited understanding or a partial/incomplete understanding of the nature of K will allow us to know some things about a good K. Thus we can distinguish between two kinds of claims:

> In order to *completely* understand "x is a good K" one must *completely* understand the nature or function of Ks.

In order to *partially* understand "*x* is a good *K*" one must *partially* understand the nature or function of *K*s.[14]

Geach's relaxation of his original claims is thus by no means a denial of the claim that "good" and "bad" are essentially attributive. Nor does the relaxation of his original claim imply that the nature or function of a thing is irrelevant to its goodness.

The point of Geach's argument is to establish that "good" and "bad," unlike logically predicative adjectives, cannot be separated from the noun they modify. Statements of the form "*x* is good" are either semantically incomplete or are elliptical for "*x* is a good *K*," where *K* is understood as indicating a kind or substantive.

The argument is relatively simple. The consequences for metaethics are quite impressive. The best way to begin to see some of these consequences and to further elucidate the thesis that "good" is essentially attributive is by considering objections.

3 Objections

There seem to be only three types of objection that can be leveled against the argument proper[15] that Geach presents for the claim that "good" is always an attributive adjective. One type claims that while "good" is often an attributive adjective it is not always one.[16] The second type of objection claims that "good" is never an attributive adjective. Objections falling into the first type are weaker than those falling into the second. One reason for this weakness is that by claiming that "good" functions as both an attributive and a predicative adjective, this type of objection succumbs to a different argument for the claim that "good" is always attributive. If "good" is always attributive, this accounts for the seemingly semantic unity of our ascriptions of goodness to diverse things.[17] But if "good" functions as attributive and predicative, then it is unclear how these seemingly radically different functions can be unified in a way that respects the semantic data.[18] Furthermore, the attempts to provide examples of predicative uses of "good" are easily translated into an attributive use, and the converse does not hold.

The second type of objection claims that good is never an attributive adjective.[19] The objections that fall into this class do not however straightforwardly commit themselves to the claim that good is always predicative. Rather what is common to objections of this sort is the claim that the attributive use of good is parasitic on some different use of good: one that does not admit of an attributive translation. In essence, objections of this sort use Geach's own argument against him, claiming that although the attributive use is grammatically appropriate it is semantically incomplete.

The third type of objection claims that while Geach's argument may be sound it is uninteresting. According to this third kind of objection, it is plausible to suppose that at some level of specificity all adjectives are attributive. Hence, Geach's argument does not reveal anything distinctive about the nature of the adjective "good."

3.1 Type One Objections

The objections considered in this section agree that there is an attributive use of "good." However, it is not the case, according to type one objections, that the attributive use is the *only* use.

3.1.1 Objectivism

Geach's argument against the predicative function of "good" is specifically directed at objectivism[20] and prescriptivism or expressivism. Objectivists like Moore and W. D. Ross grant that there is an attributive use of "good." But, they argue, there is also a predicative use. Indeed, according to Moore the predicative use is the one that is central to ethics. Moore's chief concern is to show that moral philosophers have not paid enough attention to the questions that are central to their endeavor. One of these central questions is "What is good in itself?"[21] And, according to Moore, the things that are good in themselves have no more in common with each other than the fact that they all possess the property of goodness.[22]

Moore believes a moral philosophers' chief concern should be to explain what goodness, by itself, is. He attempts to show this by arguing that ethics is, for the most part, an attempt to explain what a good man is. Since good men are men who perform good acts, ethics is primarily in the business of explaining good conduct. Moore writes, "Ethics is undoubtedly concerned with the question what good conduct is; but, being concerned with this it obviously does not start at the beginning, unless it is prepared to tell us what is good as well as what is conduct."[23] Thus, Moore's attempt to explain the nature of the referent of "good" in the phrase "good conduct" is an example of the objectivist approach.

Geach's argument works against objectivism by showing that predicative uses of "good" license invalid arguments. Hence, the statement "That's good" is semantically incomplete if no substantive is understood. There is no simple property of goodness as the objectivists maintain.

3.1.2 Bad K to K

Alfred MacKay claims that Geach is wrong to think that "bad" is an *alienans* adjective and thus wrong to think that "bad" is attributive.[24] MacKay assumes it follows from the fact that "bad" is not *alienans* that "bad" is not attributive. But this is false. As discussed earlier, Geach's reference to *alienans* adjectives is not necessary for his claim that "bad" is attributive.

MacKay's reasons for thinking that "bad" is not *alienans* appear to stem from confusion. He writes,

> [W]e have uncovered two features that might generate attributivity for an adjective: the breakdown in entailment from the original ("*x* is an *AN*") to the two conjuncts which result from "splitting" it ("*x* is a *N*" and "*x* is *A*"); and the deviance of one of the resulting conjuncts.[25]

Taking the second feature first MacKay's point is that *alienans* adjectives like "putative" cannot stand alone grammatically. "*x* is the putative father of *y*" cannot split into "*x* is putative" and "*x* is the father of *y*" because "*x* is putative" is grammatically deviant and there is a breakdown in entailment. Thus, the two features that MacKay mentions hold for "putative" and other genuinely *alienans* adjectives.

MacKay goes on to argue that neither of the two features is present with respect to "bad." He states,

> But neither of these features obtains in "bad." "X is bad" is not grammatically deviant, and a bad argument, a bad driver, and a bad movie are, respectively, an argument, a driver, and a movie. I even think that, contrary to Geach, that bad food is food.[26]

MacKay's first point is correct. "*x* is bad" is not grammatically deviant. Of course, Geach never claimed it was. Geach's claim is that "*x* is bad" is either elliptical for "*x* is a bad *K*" or semantically incomplete. MacKay's second point is again correct and irrelevant. Geach never claims that bad food is not food. Rather Geach claims "we cannot infer e.g. that because food supports life bad food supports life."[27] This claim corresponds to the second feature of *alienans* adjectives that I pointed to above—statements true of an *N* will not necessarily be true an *N* plus *alienans*. But as I said above, strictly speaking, the fact that "*x* is a bad *K*" does not logically split into "*x* is bad" and "*x* is a *K*" is enough to warrant the claim that "bad" is attributive.

3.1.3 Good K to Just Plain Bad

Charles Pigden's paper "Geach on 'Good'" contains a number of arguments against the general view that Geach aims to defend.[28] For the purpose here I only focus on his objections to the argument proper. Pigden writes, "Nobody would deny that there *is* an attributive 'good'. . . . What *is* debatable is whether 'good' (and 'bad') are *only* used attributively".[29] Pigden argues that there are cases when "good" and "bad" are used predicatively. In fact, in some cases the attributive use may presuppose the predicative use. Here's the argument: Something can be a good *K* and nevertheless be bad. If something can be a good *K* and nevertheless be bad, then the attributive use of good *K* in this case presupposes the predicative use of "bad" in this case. Hence, the attributive use of good *K* sometimes presupposes the predicative use of "bad." Here's the example:

> I may think it [an ICBM] bad (indeed evil in the highest degree) without believing it falls short *as* an ICBM or lacks the characteristics one associates with ICBMs. It is both bad and an honest-to-goodness full blown ICBM. Hence the "bad" is not *alienans* or quasi-*alienans*. Of course the "bad" is not being used attributively here (or at least it does not seem to be) since the missile need not be a bad ICBM (indeed, it may be a very good one). But this merely confirms the existence of the predicative "bad"—the very point at issue.[30]

As we shall see, Pigden's point, though in conflict with some of the other objections, shares something in common with them. One of the objections to Geach's view claims that for some uses of "good" no suitable *K* term can be supplied in order to complete "good" or, in this case, "bad." Pigden concludes that the apparent fact that no suitable *K* term can be supplied affirms the predicative use, while others conclude that it only confirms the non-attributive use (where the class of non-attributive uses includes more than just the predicative use). Thus, one way to answer these objections is simply to argue that there is, contrary to appearances, a *K* term that is being tacitly assumed in the context when something is pronounced "good" or "bad." And the specific example that Pigden uses seems to have a *K* term readily available.

As Geach notes, we must know what something is for or know what a thing's nature is before we can say that it is either good or bad (keeping in mind the qualifications at the end of Section 1). One thing's function may itself be bad for something else. The function of an ICBM is to destroy cities and kill people. An ICBM may, as Pigden notes, fulfill its function well or poorly, thereby making it a good or bad thing according to its kind. However, if an ICBM also belongs to a kind that is uniformly bad for humans, then the ICBM can be both good according to its kind and bad according to another kind.[31]

Indeed, Geach's account appears to explain the data far better than Pigden's. Why, we should ask, is the ICBM bad? Just about every moral philosopher agrees that the moral supervenes on the non-moral. On what does the badness of the ICBM supervene? We have already been told that the ICBM is a good instance of its kind. The badness of the ICBM must supervene on something other than the properties essential for its inclusion in the missile kind. So, it looks like the badness of an ICBM supervenes on its relation to some other kind, and the most plausible kind is living things. That the badness of an ICBM is due to its relation to some other kind (that is, other than the ICBM kind) is no problem for Geach.

We can specify the various kinds at issue in the statement "Good ICBM's are bad." The most salient kinds are the missile kind and the human kind. After specifying the kinds at issue, we can then assess the claim by looking at the relationship these kinds can bear to each other in order to fix the meaning of the statement. Good members of the human kind have certain characteristics, just as good members of the missile kind have certain characteristics. When the missile kind interacts with the human kind in, for example, life-threatening ways, the missile kind threatens some of the characteristics that make members of the human kind good or that which are necessary conditions for these good-making characteristics. Hence, to say that "Good missiles are bad" is just to say that good missiles typically display characteristics that typically cause the elimination of either conditions for good-making characteristics for humans or the good-making characteristics themselves. This type of story can be repeated *mutatis mutandis* for other kind relations. Hence, it is not that ICBMs are just plain bad. Rather ICBMs are bad when brought into certain relations to other kinds, such that these relations result in bad members of the other kinds. More precisely,

> *Good to Bad Kind Interaction*: A good member of some kind K may enter into relations with some other kind K^*. Some of the relations that K enters into with K^* may be bad for members of K^* or bad for members of K.

Additionally it is important that bad members of a kind may be good for members of some other kind. For example, a slow gazelle is good for a cheetah.[32]

> *Bad to Good Kind Interaction*: A bad member of some kind K may enter into relations with some other kind K^*. Some of the relations that K enters into with K^* may be good for members of K^* or good for members of K.[33]

These analyses appear to get things right. If Pigden claims that ICBMs are bad but denies that they are bad for something, then it is not at all clear what he could mean.

I have been relying on the idea that ascriptions of goodness and badness to members of some kind are in some sense relational. In the most basic or focal sense of "good" the relation is between a member x of a kind K and the kind K. ICBMs are members of the missile kind. The missile kind has certain characteristics. A particular ICBM is a good or bad member of its kind depending on how it exemplifies the characteristics that define its kind.

Furthermore, the missile kind is itself relational. That is, part of what makes a missile a missile is its relation to something else. Obviously, being an artifact, a missile bears a certain relation to its designer. If there is no designer with such-and-such intentions, there is no missile.[34] Thus, while missiles themselves are not actions, they are necessarily dependent on actions. The dependence of artifacts on actions may be lurking in the background of Pigden's objection in the following way: ICBMs are bad to make. The focus is thus turned away from the outcome or consequences to the intentions of the designer. Once again, however, Pigden's objection fails. The making of ICBMs is bad because the intention to kill indiscriminately is a bad human intention. This is simply a special case of what I above termed bad to good kind interaction. A bad human action may result in an artifactual kind that is bad, because part of the nature of the artifactual kind is determined by the intentions of its designer(s).

3.2 Type Two Objections

Objections of this type fall into two different classes. According to the first class, "good" functions attributively but in a much different way than other attributive adjectives. Various versions of expressivism may fall into this first class. According to the second class of type two objections, every appearance of "good" functioning as an attributive adjective is elliptical for some non-attributive use.

3.2.1 Expressivism

The prescriptivist or, more broadly, the expressivist may happily endorse Geach's argument against objectivism. There is no property of goodness *simpliciter*. At this point, however, the expressivist turns Geach's argument on its head. The expressivist argues that in order to avoid rampant ambiguity it is necessary to give "good" something other than a descriptive meaning. The function of "good" is not to describe whatever it modifies but to praise it or endorse it or express some attitude of approval. The expressivist argues that if "good" is primarily descriptive, as Geach claims, then it is hopelessly ambiguous. "Good" is ambiguous because ascriptions of good to knives, trucks, people, and other kinds of things must mean different things since the things that make these various kinds good are all different.[35] For example, a knife is good if it is UVW and a truck is good if is XYZ. Hence, "good knife" means UVW and "good truck" means XYZ.[36] Since "good" cannot be ambiguous in this way, the expressivist argues that "good" is not primarily descriptive. Rather "good" is primarily expressive of some pro-attitude.[37]

There are two related replies to make. First, why single out "good" in this way? There are other adjectives that behave more or less like "good" does. That is, there are other attributive adjectives. If "good" is not primarily descriptive because of its attributive nature, then is "big" or "small" or "tall" or "short" or ... similarly not primarily descriptive?

Second, Geach claims that the expressivist argument assumes that in order for "good" to be descriptive it must be predicative. But this is false. Consider the adjectival phrase "square of...." From the facts that "square of 2" means "double of 2" and "square of 3" means "triple of 3" it does not follow that "square of" is hopelessly ambiguous. "Square of" is a predicate-forming functor. By itself it is incomplete, in need of some argument to yield a value. That is, "square of x" is incomplete apart from some value for x. The same is true of "good." "Good" is a predicate-forming functor.[38] By itself "good" is incomplete. Just as "square of" is descriptive despite its yielding radically different values for different arguments, "good" is descriptive.

3.2.2 Adjunctive Uses

Judith Jarvis Thomson's objection to Geach's account is an instance of what I have labeled type-two objections. While she objects to some of the details of Geach's account, it is important to note that she is in agreement with Geach on much else. For example, like Geach, Thomson denies that the term "good" stands for some monadic property or a property that falls within the scope of KP developments. Indeed, Thomson's reasons for rejecting various versions of Moore's objectivism are scarcely different than Geach's. She is also prepared to give a functional account of most uses of "good"; she, for the most part, endorses Geach's claim that the predicate–forming functor "good" can only take as arguments things with functions or natures.[39] Yet, despite their widespread agreement she denies that "good" is an attributive adjective (in the sense presented in this chapter). Thomson argues that the attributive account of "good" is parasitic on what she calls the adjunctive account of "good." The attributive account is semantically incomplete, according to Thomson.[40]

I shall argue that a proper understanding of function and essence supports the attributive account. Since Thomson's account is quite close to Geach's and since a complete response to her objection will take us into Chapters 3 and 4, I will present her account in some detail.

Thomson argues that all goodness is goodness in a way. Alternatively, for all x, if x is good, then x is good in a way. Or, it is not the case that there is an x such that x is good and x is not good in a way. There are two orders of ways in which a thing can be good. The first-order way of being good is the most fundamental way of being good, in that all other ways of being good somehow rest on it. A first-order way of being good is explained by Thomson as being good-plus-adjunct, where good-plus-adjunct is explained by giving a list of examples. For instance, x may be good at, good for, good to use, good with, good for us, etc. x is a first-order way of being good $=_{df}$ that x is good-plus-adjunct.

The second-order way of being good rests on but is not reducible to the first-order way of being good. More precisely, second-order ways of being good rest on but are not reducible to good-plus-adjunct form. Thomson's primary example of a second-order way of being good is a good act. Normally an act is good if it is just, or generous, or otherwise displays virtue. But a just act is not reducible to the form good-plus-adjunct. A just act is something over and above an act that is good to, good at, good with, good for use in, or good for. However, second-order ways of being good (of which a good act is an instance) rest on first-order ways of being good because for an act to possess one of the virtue properties it must be successful[41]—success and not simply intention matter when ascribing virtue properties to acts. Presumably if an act is just, then it is successful. Thus, success is a necessary but not a sufficient condition for ascriptions of virtue properties to acts. Apparently, success is a first-order way of being good. Hence, for an act to be just the act must rest on some first-order way of being good.

Goodness-for is the type of success or first-order way of being good that Thomson thinks is relevant to second-order ways of being good. A second-order way of being good rests on but is not reducible to goodness-for.[42] The moral second-order ways of being good are the virtue properties. When an act or a person possesses one of the virtue properties, that act or person is good in a second-order way. On Thomson's account, the virtues are:

> ...entirely other regarding. That is a consequence of the fact that my account of the virtues, and therefore my procedure for picking out the virtue properties, construes them as fundamentally social: that is, my account of what fixes whether a character trait is a virtue, is its effect on others.[43]

The other regarding nature of the virtues is important because it leaves Thomson's account neutral on the question whether possession of the virtues is good for their possessor. Whether or not possession of the virtues is good for their possessor, possession of the virtues must be good for others.

So far, Thomson's story is that all goodness is goodness in a way, and that there are two orders of ways in which something can be good. For all x, if x is good, then x is either good in a first-order way or good in a second-order way. Something is a moral second-order way of being good only if it possesses one of the virtue properties. Something is a first-order way of being good if it benefits some thing or person. "Intuitively, for a thing X to be good in one of the first-order ways is for X to *benefit* someone or some thing Y (which might or might not be X itself) in the appropriate way, or to be capable of doing so."[44] There are many ways that x might benefit y. X may be good to look at or to taste, or good at babysitting, or good for use in making cheesecake. Given the above analysis of first-order ways of being good, these various forms of good-plus-adjunct must benefit someone or something. Thomson focuses on cases where x is good for y, since goodness-for is what moral second-order ways of being good rest on.

Thomson provides analyses of goodness-for for artifacts, inanimate non-artifacts, and animate objects. Goodness-for artifacts depends on the artifacts' design functions. Goodness-for inanimate non-artifacts depends on people's wants. Goodness for animate objects is a bit more complicated. Some animate objects have design functions that are relevant to determining what is good for them. Thomson's example is plants. Some animate objects have design functions that are not relevant to determining what is good for them. Thomson's example is people. What is good for people depends not on their design function but on what helps them in achieving their ideal goals.

As we have seen, Geach's story attempts to show, among other things, that, contrary to objectivists, there is no property of goodness. Thomson's story attempts to show, among other things, the same. In this Geach and Thomson agree; there is no property of goodness. But, Thomson argues that Geach's story is, like Moore's, incomplete. According to Thomson, Moorean statements of the form "That's good" are incomplete. Similarly, Geachean statements of the form "x is a good K" are incomplete. Both types of statements are intelligible only in a context where the way in which the thing is good is understood. Thus Geach's thesis—that good is essentially an attributive adjective—is false. Thomson suggests some examples where "good" is used and no substantive is or can be understood. "That's good for use in making cheesecake" or "That's good for Alfred" are meaningful without a substantive being understood, and Thomson suggests that no substantive could be understood. In a parenthetical comment she writes, "In fact, for what K could it at all plausibly be thought that being good for use in making cheesecake is being a good K? For what K could it at all plausibly be thought that being good for Alfred is being a good K?"[45]

We could summarize Thomson's argument as follows: Geach's thesis—for all x, if x is good then x is a good K. Thomson's objection: there exists an x such that x is good and x is not a good K (rather x is good in a way). Hence, Geach's thesis is false. Indeed, given the charge that Geach's story is incomplete, Thomson's argument amounts to the following: Geach's thesis—for all x if x is good then x is a good K. Thomson's objection: for all x if x is good then it is not the case that x is a good K.[46] Hence, Geach's thesis is false.

I will offer two partial responses to Thomson's objection. Each response is incomplete in its own way. Filling in the gaps to these will take us into Chapters 3 and 4.

First, Thomson's story and Geach's story only apparently conflict, Thomson's claim notwithstanding. The motivation for this response is due to Thomson's analysis of first-order goodness, which in her story is the fundamental kind of goodness. According to that analysis, "Intuitively, for a thing X to be good in one of the first-order ways is for X to *benefit* someone or some thing Y (which might or might not be X itself) in the appropriate way, or to be capable of doing so."[47] She then applies this analysis to artifacts, inanimate non-artifacts, and animate objects, and the latter category is further divided to distinguish those animate objects whose design functions determine their benefit from those animate objects whose design functions do not determine their benefit.

According to Geach's story, x's goodness is determined by its nature or function. If S does not know the function of x, then S cannot understand statements of the form "x is a good K." "x is a good K" may be true, but in order for S to know this, S must know what x is for or S must know the nature of x.

But Geach's story may be reconciled with Thomson's. First, both Thomson and Geach seem to say the same thing about artifacts. For some thing x to be good for some artifact y, x must benefit y by conducing to y's design functions. Geach, it seems, would say the same thing because the function of something reveals, at least in part, what is good for it and what is not. After all, part of the point with Geach's hygrometer example is that without knowing the function of a hygrometer one cannot know what is good for a hygrometer.

Second, if it is true that inanimate non-artifacts do not have design functions, as Thomson claims, then Geach too would agree that there is nothing good *for* them (though they still may be good Ks). According to Geach, something is itself good—independent of certain extrinsic relations—only if it has a function or nature.

The third case is the most difficult. For Thomson, there are some animate objects that have design functions that determine what is good for them, and there are some animate objects that have design functions that do not determine what is good for them. All animate objects have design functions, but not all design functions are relevant to determinations of what is good for a thing. Although persons have design functions (provided by natural selection), these are not relevant to determining what is good for persons. Rather, if x is good for some person P, then x must benefit P such that x's benefiting P contributes in some way to P's realizing one of her/his ideal goals.

Geach, as we have seen, thinks that "x is a good K" meaning that x is a well-functioning member of K. Thus, for Geach some thing y is good for x only if y contributes to x's being a well functioning member of K. It seems, then, that for Geach what is good for x is determined by x's functions. Hence, if x does not have a function, nothing is good for *it* strictly speaking. Geach's claim appears to be in conflict with Thomson's claim that although persons have design function, these functions are not relevant to consideration of what is good for persons.

However, the conflict may be reconciled if we add something to Thomson's story. Geach could respond that part of the function of a person is to have ideal goals that may perhaps be in conflict with the person's design function *qua* animate object. Persons *qua* free individuals have the function of attempting to realize their ideal goals. Persons *qua* animate objects have the function to survive and reproduce, etc. Where these functions conflict, the function of persons *qua* free individuals wins.

It may be objected that this attempted reconciliation is only relevant to one first-order way in which something can be good, that is, good-for. In other words, the proposed reconciliation between Thomson and Geach only works when we are considering what is good for a human. The other first-order ways in which something can be good (e.g. good with, good at, good for use, good to) cannot be reconciled with Geach's claim that the function or nature of a human is relevant to determining whether or not someone is a good human. For example, it may be good to do all sorts of things *to* humans, or a human may be good *with* all sorts of things that are not at all related to the nature or function of a human. Furthermore, the various first-order ways of being good are not reducible to some other way of being good such that each first-order way of being good has something in common with all of the others. So it may be that the function or nature of a human is relevant with respect to some first-order ways of being good but not to each of them.

Although this objection has some initial force, I think Thomson's analysis of what makes something a first-order way of being good seriously threatens the *prima facie* force of this objection. Something has to be benefited in some way for there to be first-order goodness. Geach's story simply focuses on the thing benefited. That is, for Geach, the thing with a function or nature is what is primary. In order to know what counts as beneficial for something, we need to know its function or nature. So Thomson is right to emphasize the various first-order ways of being good, but none of this is problematic for Geach. The various first-order ways of being good do have something in common, namely being beneficial, contrary to the above objection. And according to the Geachian proposal I am developing, the common feature of first-order ways of being good is primary. There is a primary way of being good, and that way is determined by a thing's nature or function. Hence, what is good for a thing depends on the thing's function. This is precisely the account of good that we have drawn out of Geach's story. Thus, there is no real conflict.

The above response helps to show how Geach is able to address Thomson's objection that there are some things that are good where no substantive is needed. In order for the statement "That's good for use in making cheesecake" to be true, it must be that the thing referred to by "that" benefits someone or something. The benefited will be good to the degree "that" benefits it. Geach is simply focusing on the thing benefited, whereas Thomson is focusing on the thing doing the benefiting. But the difference in focus does not amount to a real conflict. Both seem to agree that something must be benefited, and both agree that something must be doing the benefiting.

Another way of looking at the proposed reconciliation is to note that Thomson is simply wrong to think that there are no kinds in the offing for some of her adjunctive uses of good. For example, the statement "That's good for use in making cheesecake" does implicitly refer to a kind—namely, the making-cheesecake kind (or something close). By examining the function of making cheesecakes we can discern things that are beneficial to the process and things that are not. Again, Geach's hygrometer example is relevant here. If we have no idea what making a cheesecake amounts to we will not have any idea as to what is good for use in making cheesecake. The notion of kind-interactionism spelled out above in response to Pigden is also relevant here.

In the case of making cheesecake we have one kind—the cheesecake kind—interacting with another kind—the utensil or ingredient or whatever kind. Presumably a good member of the latter kind may benefit the former kind.[48]

There are some problems with the proposed reconciliation. The main problem is that it seems to change Thomson's account in order to make it fit Geach's. In order to reconcile Thomson's story with Geach's we have to commit her to the claim that the most fundamental way of being good (i.e. the benefiting or being benefited way) depends on a thing's function or nature. In other words, we get reconciliation without mutual compromise. In effect, Thomson's story is compatible with Geach's only if Geach's story is more fundamental. A thing's goodness is determined by its function or nature, which in turn determines how it can be benefited (as well as how it may benefit). Hence, all of the first-order ways of being good rest on the attributive account. While Thompson may not like this outcome, it does have certain advantages.

One of the advantages of the reconciliation of Thomson and Geach is that it becomes possible to tell a more seamless story about goodness. Thomson's story is seamless to the point of human goodness. Once Thomson begins to consider humans the relevant features that make non-humans good (i.e. nature and/or function) are no longer relevant. By grounding Thomson's story in Geach's, the relevant features that make non-humans good also make humans good. Another advantage of grounding Thomson's proposal on Geach's is that Geach provides a better way to understand first-order ways of being good. Thomson says all first-order ways of being good are ways of benefiting someone or something, But the notion of "ways of benefiting" is left largely unanalyzed. By turning to natures and/or functions we can provide an analysis of benefiting.

It is important to notice where the debate with Thomson has gotten us. In terms of the semantics of "good" there does not appear to be a substantial objection. There is always a substantive lurking in the background to be supplied by the context of utterance. Furthermore, Geach's claim that some substantive is needed appears supported by all the examples that Thomson alleges show the contrary. Finally, even if, *per impossible*, there are some ways of being good such that no substantive is needed, the attributive account is more fundamental. First-order ways of being good (good-plus-adjunct) rest on—and, we can grant for the sake of argument, may not be reducible to—the attributive use of "good." Where Geach and Thomson differ then is not over the semantics of "good" but over what the semantics reveal (or presuppose). For Geach, the semantics of "good" suggest that the goodness of a thing is determined by its nature and/or function, whereas for Thomson this is true only for a subset of the things that can be good. Persons, according to Thomson, are the exception to Geach's claim. In Chapters 3 and 4 I return to some of these issues, arguing that Thomson's story concludes as it does because of an impoverished view of human nature and a false analysis of function.

3.3 Type-Three Objection

According to Michael Zimmerman ". . . Geach's tests are simply irrelevant, pointing up no essential difference between the properties expressed by 'red' and 'good' and revealing no important insights into the nature of these properties."[49] Zimmerman suggests that there is no essential difference between "red" and "good" by noting the context-dependency of both adjectives.[50] He writes, "what's red as far as Macintosh apples go may not be red as far as Red Delicious apples go."[51] Indeed, "*very many* properties are determinable (to some extent) rather than (fully) determinate, including all those just mentioned [red, visible, and poisonous]."[52] The upshot is supposed to be that in some contexts hardly any adjective passes either the splitting test or the higher-order and lower-order test. Thus, Zimmerman's objection threatens to dissolve the distinction Geach needs in order for his argument to get off the ground.[53]

There are three replies to make. First, if "red" does not behave in the way Geach thought, it does not follow that there is no difference between attributive adjectives and predicative ones. All we need to do is find an adjective that satisfies either the splitting test or the higher-order and lower-order kind test and the difference is plain. Perhaps the adjective "even" will do, as it is used in the following statement: "4 is an even number." Or perhaps "valid" in "*modus ponens* is a valid argument form."

Second, Zimmerman's examples appear to pass both tests. Consider the statement "*x* is a red Macintosh apple." This statement seems to imply that *x* is red and *x* is a Macintosh apple. The original statement appears to pass the higher-order and lower-order kind test. From "*x* is a red Macintosh apple" and "all apples are fruit" we may infer that "*x* is a red fruit."

Third, and perhaps most importantly, even if all adjectives are logically attributive (and thus the first two replies fail) the essence of Geach's positive claim still follows. According to Geach, "good" is always in need of a substantive and "red" is not. Assume that all adjectives are attributive. So, all adjectives are always in need of a substantive. Thus, contrary to Geach, "red" is always in need of a substantive. But this does nothing to Geach's main point that "good" is always in need of a substantive. Zimmerman's point *supports* the claim that all adjectives are attributive, and thus subverts his objection to Geach.

If Zimmerman's point is accepted and Geach's argument does not reveal an essential difference between "good" and "red," it simply does not follow that Geach's argument does not reveal something important about the natures of these properties. Zimmerman appears to argue as follows:

1. Both "red" and "good" are attributive.
2. If both "red" and "good" are attributive, then there is no essential difference between the types of properties expressed by "red" and the types of properties expressed by "good."
3. If there is no essential difference between the types of properties expressed by "red" and the types of properties expressed by "good," then the fact that both "red" and "good" are attributive does not reveal anything important about the natures of these properties.
4. Hence, the fact that both "red" and "good" are attributive does not reveal anything important about the natures of these properties.

The third premise is false. If all adjectives are attributive, then it is never valid to move from "x is an AN" to "x is an A" and "x is an N." That is an interesting point because the nature of whatever it is that adjectives refer to would be tied to the nature of whatever the adjective modifies. Indeed, it sounds like a vindication of a full-fledged Aristotelianism. We may conclude that nothing Zimmerman says threatens Geach's argument proper.

4 Conclusion

The attributive account is left unscathed by the objections we have considered in this chapter. There are other objections to it, to be sure, and we will attempt to address some of them in the chapters to come, but at the very least we have shown that the attributive account should be taken far more seriously than its detractors and ignorers thought. With the account firmly in place, we are ready to begin drawing out some implications. One of the most important implications is that goodness is not susceptible to KP developments. In the next chapter I will present a number of reasons to support the assertion that goodness is not susceptible to a KP account. In addition, I will begin to develop the attributive account into a much more substantive metaethical theory.

CHAPTER 3

SOME METAETHICAL IMPLICATIONS OF THE ATTRIBUTIVE ACCOUNT OF "GOOD"[1]

In Chapter 1 I argued that the two most fashionable versions of moral realism face serious problems. In Chapter 2 I began to set the stage for an alternative version of moral realism by explaining and defending the claim that "good" is an attributive adjective. In this chapter I will argue for the following conditionals:

> *No Property Claim* (NP): If "good" is attributive, then the common assumption—that goodness is a property susceptible to KP developments—is false.
>
> *Goodness Depends on Nature and/or Function Claim* (GNF): If "good" is attributive, then the goodness of a thing is, in some sense, determined by the nature and/or function of that thing.

Both theses share an antecedent that I defended in Chapter 2. In this chapter I draw out some of the implications of the claim that "good" is attributive. While there are numerous important implications of the attributive account, the three most relevant to this chapter are: (a) that the common assumption—that goodness is the sort of property that is susceptible to KP developments—is false, (b) that goodness is inextricably connected to natures and/or functions, and (c) that human goodness is unique and uniform. I will argue that (c) is a consequence of GNF and the plausible claim that humans have natures.

1 In Defense of the No Property Claim

According to the common assumption, goodness is a property. Moral naturalists identify goodness with a natural property, while moral supernaturalists identify goodness with a supernatural property. As discussed in Chapter 1, many naturalists and supernaturalists respond to the OQA by rejecting a priori property identities and embracing a posteriori property identities. Thus, according to the moral naturalist and moral supernaturalist, goodness is the type of property that is susceptible to a posteriori property identities.

But the attributive account of goodness implies that goodness cannot figure in a posteriori identities. In this section I provide six reasons for why the attributive account conflicts with the necessary a posteriori account of goodness.

1.1 From Functions

According to the attributive account, "good" is a predicate-forming functor similar to "square of." That is, the predicate "good" takes other predicates as arguments and delivers a predicate as a value. More specifically, "good" is a function from kinds (and here we are willing to be quite liberal in what counts as a kind) to magnitudes of properties.[2] By magnitudes of properties I mean the varying degrees that certain properties can have. For example, if my pen is a good pen, then it must exemplify the properties required for being a member of the pen kind to such-and-such a degree.[3] Thus, "x is a good K" describes an instance of a kind (the value of "K") that has the relevant properties—the properties required for K-hood—to such-and-such a degree.

Consider the phrase "square of." Like "good" this phrase is in need of completion. The phrase "square of" takes numbers as arguments and yields numbers as values. The phrase itself is similar to "good" in that it indicates an operation to be performed on something (the argument) and it implicitly indicates the sort of thing that it delivers once the argument has been inserted (the value). "Square of" is a function from numbers to numbers and "good" is a function from kinds to magnitudes of properties. Thus, "good" as a predicate-forming functor is similar to the functor "square of."

It is plausible to suppose that the arguments and values of some functions have essences that are knowable only a posteriori. For example, the argument "human" in "x is a good human" may very well have an essence that is knowable only a posteriori. But it is not plausible to think that the functions themselves have essences that are knowable only a posteriori. Functions simply take items from some domain and map them onto items in the range. Different domains yield different ranges and different functions yield different mapping relations. As such, one cannot identify a function with any of the arguments or values that it delivers. As an operation performed on arguments, the nature of a function is not determined empirically. Hence, functions cannot figure into necessary a posteriori identities. Since, "good" is a sort of function, it follows that it cannot figure into necessary a posteriori identities, and is thus not susceptible to KP developments.

1.2 From Intensionality

In the classic examples of the necessary a posteriori, the contexts created by necessary a posteriori statements are extensional. It is always possible to substitute one of the terms flanking the identity with an extensionally equivalent term *salva veritate*. If the appearance of "good" in some statement results in a non-extensional or intensional context, then goodness is not a property of the sort that can figure into necessary a posteriori identities.

Consider the paradigmatic synthetic property identities: water is H_2O, heat is molecular motion, temperature is mean kinetic energy, and gold is atomic number 79. Each term in the synthetic identities passes the substitutivity test. Replacing "water" with some extensionally equivalent phrase does not change the truth of the identity. For example, if we replace "water" in "water = H_2O" with the rigidified definite description "Angel's actual favorite drink," the truth-value of the identity does not change. Hence, in identity statements these terms create extensional contexts.

The same is not true with respect to "good." If it were true that "good" creates extensional contexts, then from "x is a good F" and "F is G" we should be able to infer that "x is a good G," where F and G are coextensive. Such an inference is invalid. From "Suzy is a good dancer" and "All and only dancers are violinists," it does not follow that "Suzy is a good violinist."[4] Hence, good is not extensional. This is yet further evidence that goodness cannot figure into synthetic identity statements.

1.3 From Attributivity

Consider "tall," "big," and "small." Is it plausible to suppose that these attributives can figure into necessary a posteriori identity statements? In other words, could a proposition such as "Tall is F" be necessary a posteriori? If, as seems obvious, the answer is "no," then since "good" is also attributive it is reasonable to conclude that "good" too cannot figure into necessary a posteriori identity statements. The differences between comparatives such as "tall," "big," and "small" and non-comparatives such as "good" and "bad" are not sufficient to call into doubt the claim that if one group of attributives cannot figure into necessary a posteriori identity statements, the other cannot either.

Prima facie, the main reason for thinking that comparatives cannot figure into necessary a posteriori identities has nothing to do with their being comparative. Rather, comparatives cannot enter into such identities because, taken in isolation (e.g. "that's tall"), comparatives have no semantic value (unless semantic value is implicitly provided by the context). That is, comparatives need to be completed by some reference class in much the same way that "good" needs to be completed by some kind term. The attributive nature of comparatives is the reason it is implausible to suppose that they can figure into necessary a posteriori identities. Thus, while there are differences between comparative attributives and non-comparative attributives, the differences do not appear to be relevant to our present concern.

1.4 From the Necessary A Posteriori

A fourth reason for the incompatibility between the attributive account and necessary a posteriori accounts of goodness can be seen by considering the standard form by which a posteriori necessities are derived. Kripke provides a now classic example:

> [I]f P is the statement that the lectern is not made of ice, one knows by a priori philosophical analysis, some conditional of the form "if P, then necessarily P." If the table is not made of ice, it is necessarily not made of ice. On the other hand, then, we know by empirical investigation that P, the antecedent of the conditional is true—that this table is not made of ice. We can conclude by *modus ponens*:
>
> (1) If P, then necessarily P.
> (2) P.
> (3) Therefore, necessarily P.
>
> The conclusion—"Necessarily P"—is that it is necessary that the table not be made of ice, and this conclusion is known a posteriori, since one of the premises on which it is based is a posteriori.[5]

So, (1) is knowable a priori, (2) is knowable only a posteriori, and (3) is knowable only a posteriori. If we replace P with "goodness is F" we get the following:

(1*) If goodness is F, then necessarily goodness is F.
(2*) Goodness is F.
(3*) Therefore, necessarily goodness is F.

In Chapter 1 I showed the problems that arise for attempts to argue that (2*) is knowable only a posteriori. And if (2*) is not knowable only a posteriori, then the conclusion cannot be a necessary a posteriori truth. From the fact, if it is one, that (2*) is not knowable only a posteriori, it does not follow that (2*) is knowable a priori. It may be the case that (2*) is not knowable at all. For example, if (2*) does not express a proposition, then (2*) is not knowable.

According to the attributive account, (2*) does not express a proposition. If the semantics of "good" mirrors (or does something similar to mirroring) the metaphysics of goodness, then one cannot meaningfully split the property of goodness from what bears the property of goodness. But (2*) appears to assume that one can split the property of goodness from the thing that bears the property. Thus, in order to accept (2*), one must assume that the attributive account is false, and this is enough to show that the attributive account is incompatible with a posteriori necessity accounts.

1.5 From the Necessary A Posteriori (Again)

The claim of this section is that the attributive account of "good" implies that a posteriori property identities involving goodness are impossible. For the purpose of *reductio* assume that this is false. Assume that the attributive account of "good" is compatible with an a posteriori property identity involving goodness. For ease of exposition, let us assume that "goodness is F" is a true, necessary a posteriori property identity, and let us call this necessary a posteriori statement G. In order for G to be true, goodness cannot be analytically equivalent to F nor can the identity between goodness and F be discoverable a priori. The fact that G is true is thus discoverable by empirical means only. But to discover by empirical means that goodness is F, it is necessary that goodness have an essence.

Scott Soames expresses the same point.[6] According to Soames, the following route to the necessary a posteriori is the only sound route provided by Kripke; Soames calls it The Essentialist Route to the Necessary A posteriori (ERNA):

> Let p be a true proposition that attributes a property (or relation) F to an object o (or series of objects), conditional on the object (or objects) existing (while not attributing any further properties or relations to anything). Then, p will be an instance of the necessary *a posteriori* if (a) it is knowable *a priori* that F is an essential property of o, if F is a property of o at all (or a relation that holds essentially of the objects, if F holds of them at all), (b) knowledge of o that it has F, if it exists (or of the objects that they are related by F, if they exist) can only be had *a posteriori*, and (c) knowing p involves knowing of o (or of the objects) that it (they) have F, if it (they) exist at all. (o can be an individual or a kind.)[7]

The crucial thing to notice is that, according to Soames, a posteriori property identities are true only if the property flanking the right side of the identity is essential to the property or object flanking the left side of the identity. Hence, in order for the statement "goodness is F" to be true, F must express properties that are essential to goodness. Statements of the form "water is H" must express an identity that holds between water and H, such that H expresses properties that are essential to water. Thinking of the notion of a posteriori property identities in this way helps to bring out how the a posteriori property identity account of goodness cannot be correct if the attributive account of "good" is correct.

In order for goodness to figure into a posteriori identities, it must have an essence that can only be discovered empirically. But it is plausible to suppose that in order to discover the essence of goodness empirically, goodness must be separable from the things that it modifies. In other words, the supposition that goodness is susceptible to KP analysis assumes the falsity of the attributive account.

To see that one must assume the falsity of the attributive account to make sense of the a posteriori account, consider the property of redness. It is plausible to suppose that redness has an essence only discoverable a posteriori because it is plausible to suppose that the redness of a thing can be discovered independently of the thing that is red. In other words, it is possible to know that something is red without being able to identify the thing that is red. The redness of a thing does not depend on the thing that is red in the way that the goodness of a thing depends on the thing that is good. But the fact that the nature of red is independent of what it qualifies appears to imply that the redness of things can be empirically investigated apart from investigating the things that are red. That is, the possibility of there being an a posteriori identity of the form "redness is F" assumes that it is possible to empirically investigate redness (in such a way that the nature of the thing that is red is irrelevant to the nature of redness). Generalizing from the red case, the following seems to be a necessary condition for the possibility of a property having a nature that is discoverable only a posteriori:

> *Necessary Condition for A Posteriori Identities* (NCA): If F is a property with a nature that is only discoverable *a posteriori*, then the nature of F must not depend on the thing(s) that F modifies.

If we substitute goodness for F, it is easy to see why the attributive account and NCA are incompatible. NCA states that properties susceptible to KP analysis have natures that do not depend on the things that instantiate the property. Thus, the nature of redness (if susceptible to KP analysis) is independent of the nature of anything that is red. The attributive account states that it is not possible for "good" to be separated from the thing that it modifies. The nature of goodness is dependent on the nature of the thing that is good. Hence, given the truth of the attributive account of "good" it follows that goodness does not fall within the scope of a KP analysis.

1.6 From Adverbialism

Perhaps, the most promising line of argument for the claim that goodness cannot figure into synthetic property identities is simply that, in order for goodness to do so, it would have to be detachable from what it modifies. Since "good" is not detachable from what it modifies, goodness cannot figure into synthetic property identities (again assuming that the semantics mirrors the metaphysics to some degree). In the previous two sections I considered this line of argument by focusing on the nature of a posteriori necessities. In this section I consider this line of argument by focusing on the nature of the attributive account. It will be helpful to consider an analogy between the attributive account of "good" and adverbial theories of mental states.

According to the adverbial theory of mental states, statements of the form "John has an itch" are grammatically misleading. The grammatical form of "John has an itch" is similar to the grammatical form of "John has a car." In the latter sentence, the subject is John and the object is a car. The similarity between these two sentence forms leads many to think of both cars and itches as objects capable of existing on their own. The adverbialist denies the inference from "John has an itch" to "Itches can exist on their own," but not from "John has a car" to "Cars can exist on their own." The similarity in grammatical form does not warrant the inference to similarity in logical form, and hence does not warrant the inference to similarity in ontological form. In other words, statements of the grammatical form "S-V-O" (where S stands for subject, V for verb, and O for object) do not imply that there is a subject and there is an object. In the case of the statement "John has an itch," there are no such things as itches existing independently of the subjects that have them. As Michael Tye puts it, "Any pain or itch or image is always *somebody's* pain or itch or image."[8]

Michael Loux has drawn a similar analogy between adverbialism and Aristotle's claim that only substances exist. *Prima facie*, statements such as "Plato believes that Fido is a dog" suggest that Plato stands in the believing relation to something usually said to be a proposition. In order to square Aristotle's claim that only substances exist, the Aristotelian needs to explain away the commitment that propositional attitudes appear to have to the existence of propositions. In other words, like the attributive account of "good" and the adverbial account of mental states, the Aristotelian account needs to show that surface grammar is misleading in statements that appear to commit one to the existence of other things beside substances. Loux writes,

> [H]ere the Aristotelian has characteristically argued that the surface grammar of intentional discourse is misleading. It suggests a relational interpretation of conceptual activity, where we have a mental state or act a person undergoes and an object that the state or act takes ... The Aristotelian insists on rejecting this act-object interpretation in favor of what is often called the act theory of intentionality, according to which expressions like "believes that Fido is a dog" and "thinks that 2 + 2 = 4" are construed not in relational terms but as one-place predicates enabling us to say how it is with persons.[9]

Loux goes on to suggest that Aristotelians construe propositional attitude reports in the same way that adverbialists construe perceptual reports. He states, "One obvious form the act theory can take involves an adverbial account of intentional discourse where the recalcitrant that-clauses are construed as adverbs expressing *how* a person thinks, conceives, believes, and so on."[10] Rather than being committed to the existence of propositions, the act theorist, like the adverbialist, can argue that propositions, like itches, do not enjoy an existence on their own. In the statement "Plato believes/thinks/conceives/etc. that Fido is a dog" the subject Plato is in a certain mental state. The only thing that exists is Plato. The statement simply "expresses how [Plato] thinks, conceives, believes, and so on."

Loux suggests another way for the Aristotelian to explain away the misleading surface grammar. He writes, "Alternatively, the act theorist can deny that verbs like 'believes' and 'conceives' are complete predicates, construing them, say, as predicate-forming functors that take declarative sentences as their arguments and yield as their values one-place predicates true or false of persons."[11] This analysis is quite similar to the attributive account of "good." Like the attributive account of "good," the predicate-forming functor analysis of propositional attitudes claims that verbs such as "believes" and "conceives" do not relate persons to objects but rather describe persons.

The attributive account of "good" claims that statements like "That's good" are incomplete. In keeping with Loux's terminology, the attributive account claims that "good" is a predicate-forming functor that takes kinds as arguments and yields as values one-place predicates that are either true or false of particular instances of the appropriate kind. Hence, "good," like "believes" on the predicate-forming functor account, does not relate things to the property goodness. Rather, "good" describes things without itself referring to some unique property.

Each of the above elaborations on the attributive account of "good" implies that it is a mistake to think that goodness could figure into a posteriori necessities. First, there is no property of goodness that exists apart from the kind it modifies. If it were possible to provide a synthetic property identity for goodness, goodness would have to be a property existing independently of the thing it modifies (or have a nature that is not intimately connected to the nature of the thing it modifies). The attributive account implies that "good" is inseparable from the noun it modifies. Second, "good" is something like a predicate-forming functor. It is by itself incomplete. Since "good" requires completion by a kind term, the function of "good" is to describe the kind term it modifies, similar to the way that Loux suggests propositional attitudes describe the persons they modify.

In this section, I have argued that "good" does not refer to a property of the sort needed by moral realists who maintain that goodness is a property and that the nature of goodness may be knowable only a posteriori. Indeed the function of "good" is nothing like the function of terms referring to properties. In the case of "x is a red o," the statement tells us that o belongs to the set of red things. In the case of "x is a good K," the statement does not tell us that x belongs to the set of good things. Rather the statement tells us that x is a K, and x has the attributes required for membership in K to such-and-such a degree. In other words, a thing's being a good K is somehow connected to the nature of Ks. The next section attempts to make this connection explicit.

2 Second Implication of Attributive Account: Goodness, Natures, and Functions

The attributive account of "good" implies that only things with natures or functions can be good.[12] Nearly every commentator on the attributive account assumes that it implies only things with natures or functions can be good (hereafter, I will eliminate "and/or" and use just "or," to be read as inclusive). In Chapter 2, I pointed out that one objection to the attributive account arises from the apparent fact that things without natures or functions can be good. In this section, I argue that the attributive account does imply that only things with natures or functions can be good, but that this is not a problem. A full defense against the objection that things without natures or functions can be good is provided in Chapter 4.

The attributive account of "good" rules out the KP gambit. The inseparability of "good" from the noun it modifies implies both that goodness is not the sort of thing that can figure into synthetic property identities, and suggests that any correct understanding of goodness must include an account of the type of thing to which goodness is being attributed. In other words, a correct understanding of the statement "x is a good K" requires understanding something about the modifier, "good," and the modified, "K." This is as it should be. In the last chapter, I appealed to the notions of function and nature or essence in order to dispel various worries. Although different types of things can be good, what makes different types of things good is determined by the natures or functions of the things.

The goodness of a thing is determined by its nature or function. If x is a member of some kind K, then x is a good K iff x is a functioning member of K to such-and-such a degree.[13] This definition is silent on the issue of the primary K a thing belongs to. Thus, the following could very well be true: everything is a good member of some kind. Surely it is possible that each thing is a good member of some kind or other. The book on the shelf may be a bad book, but a good doorstop. The man on the stage may be a bad actor but a good violinist. Context will often determine the salient kind, but it is not all up to context. The nature of a thing determines the thing's primary kind.[14] *War and Peace* is most fundamentally a member of the book kind or the fiction book kind. It is only secondarily a member of other kinds. What we need, then, is a way to determine the primary kind that a thing belongs to. My suggestion is that natures will help here.

Kit Fine provides compelling reasons to think that a thing's nature or essence is not coextensive with a thing's unique necessary properties.[15] Fine gives the example of Socrates and the singleton set {Socrates}. The singleton {Socrates} is a necessary property of Socrates. There is no possible world in which Socrates exists and the singleton does not.[16] Nevertheless, Fine argues, it is implausible to suppose that the singleton is essential to Socrates. The singleton reveals nothing about the essence or nature of

Socrates. Hence, necessary properties, even those that are unique to the individual, are not necessarily essential. From these considerations Fine suggests that the essence of a thing is its definition (understood in the ancient and medieval sense) where a definition is the fundamental genus and differentiating species of a thing. For example, the most fundamental genus and differentiating species to which humans belong has been thought to be rational animal.

Michael Rea has recently provided the following definition of a thing's primary kind.[17]

> K is x's *primary kind* $=_{df}$ x belongs to K and any term that refers to K is a (metaphysically) better answer to the question "What kind of thing is x?" than any term that does not refer to K.[18]

For example, if asked "What kind of thing is Julian?" the answer "He is a human," is better than the answer "He is an animal" or "He is an organism." Each answer is correct, but the first provides the most fundamental or primary kind to which Julian belongs. Rea's suggestion nicely elaborates Fine's. Thus, the definition of a thing (in Fine's sense) corresponds to a thing's primary kind (in Rea's sense).

Using Fine's distinction between essence and necessary properties, we can now say that a thing's most fundamental kind is identical to its essence or nature. With the distinction between fundamental kind and non-fundamental kind in hand, we can explain how it is possible for a thing x to be both a good K and a bad K' and a bad K but a good K'. Where K designates a thing's most fundamental kind and K' designates a thing's non-fundamental kind, it is easy to see how, for example, a lawnmower might be a good lawnmower (K) and a bad piece of yard furniture (K') or a good piece of yard furniture and a bad lawnmower (of course it could also be a good lawnmower and a good piece of lawn furniture).[19] Lawnmower's most fundament kind is revealed by its essence or nature.[20] In the case of artifacts, it is plausible to suppose that the essence of an artifact just is its function. Hence, the essence of a lawnmower is a machine that cuts grass. If a specific lawnmower does not cut grass efficiently, then it is a bad lawnmower. The same sort of thing could be said for non-human animals. While non-human animals are not artifacts and thus identifying their natures with their function is perhaps implausible, the essence or nature of a non-human animal determines to some degree its goodness. Since the essence of a rabbit is different from the essence of a horse, a good rabbit will necessarily possess different features from a good horse.

The above account of the distinction between natures and necessary properties provides us with the means to specify the most fundamental kind to which a thing belongs. Doing so allows us to distinguish between a thing's being a good member of its most fundamental kind and a thing's being a good member of some other non-fundamental kind. In certain cases such as non-human animals (I leave the discussion of human animals for the third section of this chapter) and plants, a thing's nature is not identical to its function, though the two are intimately related.[21]

Consider, for example, the function of a heart. The function of a heart is to pump blood. If the function of a heart and the nature of a heart were identical, then anything with the property of pumping blood (the function of the heart) would be identical to a heart. But clearly this is not so. Is an artificial heart a heart? How about a machine that pumps blood for the person hooked up to it? The natural answer to both questions seems to be "no." An artificial heart is, well, an artificial heart, not a heart, just as artificial leather is not leather.[22] Someone has an artificial heart because her/his heart has stopped functioning as it ought. But if the function of a heart is identical to its nature, it would not make sense to say that the person's heart stopped functioning so she/he now has an artificial heart. Rather, we should say that her/his heart stopped functioning so she/he now has a new heart. But upon hearing the latter claim, we would normally suppose that the person underwent a heart-transplant, not that she/he had received an artificial heart. Hence, the nature of certain kinds (e.g. natural kinds as opposed to artifactual kinds) is not identical to their function.[23]

Despite the fact that the nature of certain kinds is not identical to their function, natures and functions are nevertheless intimately related. Consider again a heart. Let N designate the nature of a heart and F its function. N and F are not identical. Something can have F for its function but not N as its nature. That is, something can have pumping blood as its function without being a heart (e.g. an artificial heart or an external machine). Does the converse hold? That is, can something have N as its nature without having F as its function? It seems not. If a heart's nature is N, then its function is F. The nature of a heart determines or includes its function. The relationship between natures and functions helps explain how it makes sense to say that a given heart is a bad heart. If x is a bad heart, x nevertheless is a heart; a bad heart is still a heart. In every possible world in which hearts exist, they are N. The distinction between a bad heart and a good heart is, thus, not a distinction between the natures of various hearts. Rather, it is a distinction between the various hearts' degrees of functioning. A bad heart is one that does not function as it should; it is not functioning according to its nature. A good heart is one that does function as it should, as its nature determines. Hence, x is a good K, where K is the most fundamental kind that x belongs to, iff x is a properly functioning member of K. Hence, the attributive account implies that things without functions or natures cannot be good.[24]

2.1 Objections

J. J. Thomson and others have noted that, strictly speaking, the attributive account does not rule out attributing goodness to things that do not have functions.[25] For example, "x is a good pebble" or "x is a good corpse" appear to satisfy the desiderata revealed by the attributive account. But, since we are prompted to ask, "a good pebble for what?" or "a good corpse for what?," such statements do not make sense; they are semantically incomplete, requiring some adjunctive phrase in order to complete them, argue Thomson and others. Thus, "x is a good pebble for breaking windows" or "x is a good corpse for anatomy" make sense. According to these philosophers, the attributive account licenses incomplete statements, and thus, the attributive account should be replaced by the adjunctive account, which does not appear to have the same consequence.

There are at least two responses to the above objection. I will postpone the second response until the next chapter, where we will cover the metaphysics of function in some detail. The first response states that the semantic incompleteness found by Thomson and others is based on a misunderstanding. The attributive account begins by saying that "good" cannot be separated from the "substantive" (to use Geach's term) or the noun it modifies. The attributive account need not end there (and Geach's does not). The substantive's nature is relevant to determining whether or not it can properly occupy the argument position in the incomplete statement "x is a good." The suggestion of this section is that only things with natures or functions can properly fill the argument position. Since there is no natural or conventionally understood function of pebbles or corpses, the phrases are odd. The fact that statements such as "x is a good pebble" or "x is a good corpse" sound odd or even absurd is nicely explained.

Jyl Gertzler defends a Socratic account of goodness along the same lines. According to Socrates, there is a good and a bad for each thing.[26] Socrates' claim seems absurd when applied to pebbles and corpses. What, we wonder, could benefit a pebble or a corpse? Gertzler provides the following response:

> While Socrates suggests that there is a "good and a bad for each thing", it might seem that there are some types of things—e.g., a pile of trash, the smallest elementary particle [pebbles and corpses]—for which it is impossible to conceive of benefits or harms. But these cases, one might argue, are the very exceptions that prove the rule, since the first is a case of something that fails to count as a genuine thing . . ., and the second is a case of something whose unity is always guaranteed (and so cannot be benefited or harmed). I suspect that our hesitation to agree with Socrates' suggestion that things can be good for wood or bad for iron is due to the fact that the "stuffs" of wood and iron lack sufficient unity to count as genuine things. Once we have in mind a particular wooden or iron thing, say, a statue, we are no longer at a loss to think of things that might count as good or bad for it.[27]

Gertzler's main concern is to defend the idea that the oneness or unity of a thing provides a criterion of evaluation. While that is not my concern, her remarks are relevant to the attributive account. It may be that neither pebbles nor corpses are genuine things and, thus, cannot have a nature or function. Hence, a good pebble or a good corpse is simply a category mistake. Or it may be that pebbles and corpses have natures or functions, but that they are guaranteed to fully realize them. If pebbles and corpses are guaranteed to realize their natures (or to fulfill their functions), then they cannot be benefited or harmed. Thus, nothing could count as being good or bad for a pebble or a corpse. Furthermore, a good pebble would just be a pebble. The fact that a pebble always fully realizes its nature or function would imply that simply being a pebble entails being a good one. The redundancy helps explain the oddity in the claim that this is a good pebble.[28]

To many, the implication that only things with functions or natures can be good is a *reductio* of the attributive account. Two different types of counterexample are often cited as posing problems for this implication. First, there are things with functions that may be good, but this fact is not due to their proper functioning. An example often cited is humans. John, it is claimed, may be a good human, despite the fact that John is not a properly functioning human.[29] Another example is news.[30] The statement "That's good news." does not refer to the function of news. Second, there are things without functions that can be good. For example, it seems perfectly intelligible to say, "that is a good sunset" and the statement does not appear to have anything to do with the function or nature of sunsets.[31]

According to the first type of counterexample, there are some things that are good independently of their function. That is, some member x of kind K may have function F and x may be a good K despite the fact that x does not perform F well. Thus, the performance of a function is, in some cases, irrelevant to its goodness. The function of news is to convey information not previously known. But, it is urged, something can be good news despite the fact that the function of news is not properly executed.

It is important to notice that the *good news* objection (as we might call it) trades on an ellipsis. Whenever someone claims "That's good news." the statement is elliptical for something like "That's good news for me." or "That's good news for you." or "That's good news for such and such." These statements make explicit that what is good is not the news qua news (i.e. the conveyance of previously unknown information) but the content of the news. The news is good news not because of its presentational features but rather because the content is in some sense beneficial to someone (or some collection of beneficiaries).[32] If the news is indeed good news, then it must be good for someone or something. As we have seen in Chapter 2 and will explore in the next section, whether or not something is good for someone depends on the nature or function of humans. Thus, contrary to the objection, something's function *is* relevant for determining the truth of the claim "That's good news."

The second type of counterexample claims that it is possible for things without functions to be good. Other than the first reply given below, the replies to this type of counterexample hold, *mutatis mutandis* for every instance, so I will focus on just one example. Consider the claim that some sunset is good. The claim appears to be a counterexample, because sunsets do not have functions, and yet some are good and some are bad. Thus, it is false that only things with functions can occupy the argument place in "*x* is a good _____."

First, it is worth pointing out that the statement "That is a good sunset." is not often heard. Instead, "That is a beautiful sunset." or "That is a pretty sunset." or some other statement involving terms that are more response-dependent than "good" is usually offered. Second, the statement "That's a good sunset." usually means that the sunset is good for viewing or good for drawing or good for. . . . The "good for" construction will be dealt with in a bit more detail in Chapter 4. For now it is enough to point out that "good for" constructions do not threaten the attributive account, because it is plausible to suppose that there is something with a function that is relevant to determining the truth-value of the claim.

So far we have discussed artifacts, plants, and non-human animals. We have seen that in the artifact case, the function of an artifact is (or may be) identical to its nature. In the plant and animal cases, natures and functions should probably be distinguished. Nevertheless, in the plant and non-human animal cases, natures and functions are intimately related. Natures determine (or include) functions, and functions determine the goodness or badness of a thing. It is now time to consider humans.

3 Third Implication of Attributive Account: Good Humans

The attributive account of "good," together with GNF and the plausible assumption that humans have a nature implies that human goodness is unique and uniform. If *S* is a human, then there is one and only one good for *S* qua human.[33] For many moral philosophers, this implication is reason enough for them to reject the attributive account of "good" or to argue that the attributive account does not imply that human goodness is unique and uniform.[34] I argue that the claim that human goodness is unique and uniform does follow from the attributive account of "good," together with GNF and the claim that humans have a nature. Second, I argue that this implication is a virtue of any moral theory, and that the objections raised against it are based either on thin accounts of human nature or on a misunderstanding of the claim that human goodness is unique and uniform.

For each thing with a nature or essence, there is a fundamental kind to which that thing belongs (for all *x*, if *x* has a nature, then there is a *K* such that *K* is the most fundamental kind to which *x* belongs). Indeed, the fundamental kind to which a thing belongs is just its nature or essence, given Fine's work. Humans belong to a kind. Each human is a member of the same fundamental kind. Let us call the fundamental kind to which humans belong RA (for rational animal). RA is the nature of each member of the human kind. In order for x to be a member of the human kind, x must be a rational animal. Since we have already shown that the goodness of a thing depends on the nature or function of that thing, it follows that the goodness of a human depends on a human's nature or function.

According to the attributive account of "good", "good" cannot, logically, be separated from the noun it modifies. As we have seen, the noun which "good" modifies must be a noun that refers to a kind.[35] However, not just any kind will do. Gerrymandered kinds that do not cut nature at its joints will, often, not work because the members of these kinds do not have functions or natures.[36] Thus, "good" must modify kinds whose members have functions or natures. A simple—perhaps too simple—argument gets us to the desired conclusion. It is perfectly intelligible to talk of good humans. Hence, human kind has members that have a nature or function. Given GNF, the goodness of a thing is, in some sense, determined by its nature or function. Hence, the goodness of a human is determined, in some sense, by the nature or function of humans. Given that humans have one nature and that this nature determines what a good human (qua human) is it follows that human goodness is unique and uniform. Human goodness is unique because human nature is unique. Human goodness is uniform because each thing that has the nature of a human is essentially a human. That is, the property being human is both necessary and essential to anything that has it (drawing on Fine's distinction between necessary properties and essential ones discussed above).

There are many objections that can be raised against the claim that human goodness is unique and uniform. Considering these objections and the responses will help to clarify that claim.

3.1 Objections

As we shall see, the most pressing problem for theories that attempt to ground morality in human nature has to do with the diversity through which humans seem to be able to express that nature. The worry is that there are many forms that human goodness can take, and that only a small number of these forms are grounded in human nature. The objections that we shall consider in this section can all be seen as species of this more general concern.

3.1.1 The Gauguin Problem

Bernard Williams raises an interesting problem for theories of morality that appeal to human nature.[37] We can, felicitously, recast Williams's argument in the form of a dilemma.[38]

(1) Either human nature determines a set of moral standards that collectively pick out one way of life as exemplifying that nature or it does not.
(2) If human nature does determine a set of standards that collectively pick out one way of life as exemplifying that nature, then it is likely that the way of life picked out will not have much to do with morality (and thus human nature is not grounding morality).
(3) If human nature does not determine a set of standards that collectively pick out one way of life as exemplifying that nature, then human nature is not grounding morality.
(4) Hence, human nature does not ground morality.

Williams calls this the *Gauguin Problem* because the life of a creative genius seems to exemplify human nature to a high degree, but such a life may not have much or anything to do with morality.[39] Indeed, such a life may conflict with morality. As Williams puts it:

> A moralist who wants to base a conception of the right sort of life for man on considerations about the high and distinctive powers of man can scarcely disregard the claims of creative genius in the arts or sciences to be included preeminently among such powers; yet he will find it hard to elicit from, or even reconcile with, an ideal of the development and expression of such genius, the more everyday and domesticated virtues and commitments of which morality has to give some account.[40]

There are, at least, two responses to be given to the *Gauguin Problem*. Consider the following parody argument:

(1*) Either the nature (or function) of a time-keeping device (e.g. a watch or a clock) determines a set of standards that collectively pick out one way of exemplifying that nature, or its nature (or function) does not.
(2*) If the nature of a time-keeping device does determine a set of standards that collectively pick out one way of exemplifying that nature, then it is likely that the way picked out will not have much to do with how time-keeping devices ought to behave.
(3*) If the nature of a time-keeping device does not determine a set of standards that collectively pick out one way of exemplifying that nature, then the nature of a time keeping device is not grounding how time-keeping devices ought to behave.
(4*) Hence, the nature of a time-keeping device does not ground how time-keeping devices ought to behave.

For convenience we will call the parody argument the *Watch Problem*. That the *Watch Problem* is no problem at all is fairly obvious. (2*) seems clearly false. The nature of a time-keeping device is to tell time. A time-keeping device may tell time poorly or it may tell time well. If a time-keeping device tells time poorly, then it is a bad time-keeping device and if it tells time well, then it is a good time keeping device.[41] The nature of a time-keeping device not only determines a set of standards that collectively pick out one way of exemplifying the nature of a time-keeping device, it also determines how time-keeping devices ought to behave.

While the nature of a time-keeping device does determine how a time-keeping device ought to behave, the nature does not specify each and every detail about how specific time-keeping devices ought to be. For example, a good time-keeping device may be a clock or a watch. It may be large or small, made of plastic or metal or wood. In other words, while the nature determines a kind of homogeneity at one level, it does not rule out heterogeneity at other levels.[42]

Returning to Williams's argument, we can now locate the problem in the second premise. Human nature (whatever it is) can specify a distinctive and uniform kind of goodness that is perfectly compatible with the artistic genius and with the "more everyday and domesticated virtues and commitments of which morality has to give some account." The primary kind to which the artist or factory worker belongs is the human kind. If the artist or factory worker flouts the standards (and Williams recognizes that there are standards associated with human kind) associated with being human, then she is a bad member of her kind. The non-primary kinds to which the artist or factory worker belongs will, no doubt, also provide standards of evaluation. As we layer these non-primary kinds upon each other, a much more substantive ethics emerges. The main point of the response to Williams's objection is that the primary kind provides standards of evaluation that must be met by any good member of the kind. That the standards of evaluation picked out by the primary kind do not specify every requirement that members of the kind must meet should be seen as a virtue of the theory, not a vice.

Second, Williams's argument may rest on a thin account of human nature. Indeed, I suspect that many of the objections to moral theories, such as the one presented here, rely on a thin account of human nature. The thinner the account, the more difficult it will be to ground morality on it.

Williams worries that artistic geniuses will either be left out of the moral picture or artistic geniuses will force us to leave out the main concerns of morality. His worry appears to rest on the assumption that the artistic or creative genius exemplifies human nature better than anyone.[43] It does not appear as though the structure of the moral theory presented here would in any way commit us to the claim that creative genius is the highest expression of human nature any more than the nature of a time keeping device commits one to the claim that a Rolex is the highest expression of time keeping nature.

3.1.2 The Argument from Agreement

R. M. Hare, I am told, has noted that any theory of human goodness that claims that some human is a good member of its kind just in case it fulfills the function of humans to such-and-such a degree fails from the start since we know what it means to be a good human without knowing what the function or nature of a human is.[44] Geach appears to think otherwise. He writes, "If I do not know what hygrometers are for, I do not really know what 'hygrometer' means, and *therefore* do not really know what 'good hygrometer' means; I merely know that I could find out its meaning by finding out what hygrometers were for. . . ."[45] Though Geach here talks of artifacts, his point is, I take it, meant to generalize to non-artifacts as well. If we do not know what humans are for, we will not really know what "human" means, and therefore will not really know what "good human" means. Most, I assume, will find the substitution of humans for hygrometers preposterous. Perhaps in order to know the meaning of a term that refers to an artifact we must know what the artifact is for, but granting this requirement in no way commits one to the view that in order to know what the term "human" means one must know what humans are for. We can break the present objection into two parts: (a) Geach is wrong to suppose that the meaning of a term is somehow intimately connected to the nature of the thing to which the term refers, and (b) Geach is wrong to suppose that we must know the function or nature of a thing before we can judge it good or bad.

First, it is important to remember the effect that the qua-problem had on the pure causal theory of reference. If the qua-problem is indeed a problem and the hybrid solution is indeed the only way to save the causal theory of reference, then for many terms (especially natural kind terms) the meaning of the term will include at least a partial understanding of the nature of the referent.[46] According to the hybrid theory of reference, in order initially to baptize the natural kind tiger when confronted with an instance of tiger one must have some necessarily true description in mind. The description cannot be too general, lest the qua-problem reemerge. Thus, the description must be such that it includes at least part of what it is to be a member of the tiger kind. The term "tiger," then, does not refer without any descriptive content. Rather, it refers with *some* content, specifying at least one characteristic tigers have that demarcates them from non-tigers. Such a description is, it seems, at least a partial specification of the nature of tiger. If this account is correct, then Geach is not as far off as (part (a)) to the above objection implies. Terms that refer to things that have natures must include in their meaning at least a partial specification of the nature of the referent.

But if the meaning of a term must include a partial specification of the nature of the referent, the fact that in some cases the nature is identical with the function would imply that the meaning of the term sometimes includes (at least partially) the thing's function.[47] That the meaning of a term includes the referent's function is not implausible with respect to artifactual terms. The meaning of "hygrometer" just is whatever hygrometers are for. But what about the term "human"? The meaning of "human" does not appear to have anything to do with the function—if there is one—of humans.

Again, the hybrid theory may help here. The initial baptism of the species "human" could not have been a purely causally referential one, given that the qua-problem is a problem and the hybrid theory is the best solution. The initial baptism must have included at least a partial specification of the nature of the referent. However, since natures and functions are not identical in the case of organisms, it does not follow that the meaning of "human" is constituted in part by the function of human. What we now have is the following: if we do not know what humans are (even partially), we will not really know what "human" means, and therefore will not really know what "good human" means. It appears that part (a) to the objection has been met; the meaning of a term is, at least partially, related to the nature of the thing the term refers to.

Part (b) to the objection claims that we can truly judge of x that it is a good K without knowing what Ks are or what Ks are for. Geach's hygrometer example is again relevant here, as are examples of other artifacts. In the case of "good humans," the nature of a human must still be grasped, at least partially, in order for us to know what it is to be a good human. In Chapter 2, I noted that if we do not need to know anything at all about the natures of humans in our evaluations, then we could not know whether justice or temperance or courage are indeed good-making characteristics. At least some rudimentary knowledge about what humans are is necessary for determining whether x is a good human. Furthermore, at least rudimentary knowledge of what humans are is necessary for determining whether y is good for humans.

Nevertheless, Hare and others may persist: we simply do not know what human nature is in anything more than a rudimentary way, and we have no idea what the function of a human is. But we do know what a good human is.

The claim that we do not know either the nature or function of humans is, I think, false. However, responding to Hare's objection adequately does not depend on the latter claims' falsity. If we grant that we do not know what the function of a human is, we can *use* this fact to account for widespread moral disagreement. If we can account for widespread moral disagreement, then one of the major obstacles to moral realism is removed.

One of the major objections to moral realism is that the type of disagreement we find in morality is different from the type of disagreement we find in science. In science, disputes are often settled. In morality, disputes are rarely settled. We seem to have well-defined procedures for adjudicating scientific debates, which appears to be lacking in debates about morality. The discrepancy between moral and non-moral disagreement is then cited as evidence that ethics does not deal with an objective reality. According to the version of moral realism being offered here, however, the discrepancy is easily explained. Given that human goodness depends on the nature or function of humans and that there is little agreement on what the nature and function of a human is, it is not surprising to find so much moral disagreement. Until we agree that humans are such-and-such or have function so-and-so, we will never agree on less basic moral issues.[48] Thus, the moral theory advocated here nicely explains the nature of moral disagreement in a way that is consistent with moral realism.

Being able to explain moral disagreement in terms of disagreement over the nature or function of a human helps to dissolve Hare's objection. The fact that the moral theory advocated here explains such phenomena, where other theories fail, helps to increase its plausibility. Thus, human nature is relevant and the claim that human goodness is dependent on human nature and human function makes perfect sense, both of our overall use of the term "good" and of one of the most significant objections to moral realism.

Hare's objection assumes that there is agreement about what features a good human would have. Is it at all plausible to suppose that if there is such agreement, the relevant features do not reveal, in part, the nature of humans? It seems the answer is no. If there is agreement about what features a good human would have, then from this agreement we can discover the nature, in part, of humans. Imagine an analogous situation in which someone does not know the nature or function of a pen but is told of some particular example that it is a good pen. Knowing facts about the pen and knowing that the pen is a good one would enable the individual to discover the nature or function of pens. Similarly, knowing that a particular person is a good human would enable us to discover the nature of a human. Does this imply it is false that morality is grounded in human nature? Not at all! To say that our knowledge of the features required for being a good human reveals the nature of a human is epistemological. To say that morality is grounded in human nature is metaphysical. The claim that the metaphysics of morality is revealed by our moral knowledge is perfectly compatible with the claim that morality is grounded in human nature.

3.1.3 Ideal Goals

A closely related objection has been proffered by J. J. Thomson. According to Thomson, some animate objects have design functions that are not relevant to determining what is good for them. Thomson's example is humans. What is good for humans depends not on their design function but on what helps them in achieving their ideal goals. She writes, "X is good for Alfred just in case X benefits him in that it conduces to his reaching one or more of (what I shall call) his *ideal goals*."[49] Thomson's account of ideal goals is the familiar one. An ideal goal of Alfred's "is what Alfred would aim at in ideal conditions of full information about costs, assessed 'in a cool hour,' and lack of improper preference bendings."[50] Given this characterization of what benefits Alfred, Thomson concludes that Alfred's design functions may or may not aid him in achieving his ideal goals. Hence, Alfred's achieving his design functions may or may not be good for him. On this score Thomson states,

> [N]ot only do use function and role functions fail to fix what is good for a person, but so also do design functions. Suppose that Alfred was designed by nature to A. Conducing to his A-ing may conduce to his reaching one or more of his ideal goals. But it may not. Doing so may even conflict with reaching one or more of his ideal goals. If conducing to his A-ing does not conduce to his reaching an ideal goal, then the familiar theory [the theory that grounds what is good for a person in his or her achieving their ideal goals] tells us that doing so is not good for him. So design functions have not the role of fixing what is good for a person that they have in fixing what is good for artifacts.[51]

According to the theory I am advocating, x is a good K just in case x fulfills its function or nature to such-and-such a degree. Among other things, this means that x must function as befits Ks. Thomson's theory appears to be in conflict with this theory. But perhaps appearances are misleading. After all, Thomson speaks of what is good for a person and not of what a good person is. What is good for a person is whatever conduces to their achieving their ideal goals. It seems perfectly consistent to maintain Thomson's notion of goodness-for along with my notion of a good K.[52]

The problem with the attempt to reconcile the two views (granting Thomson the coherence of her account of ideal goals) is that according to my account, it should be among a person's ideal goals to be a good human. To see why, consider the standard account of a human's nature: the standard account tells us that humans are essentially rational animals. Thus, being a good human means exemplifying one's rationality and animality to such-and-such a degree. Given Thomson's characterization of ideal goals, it seems that one of an agent's ideal goals (perhaps the ideal goal) should be a desire to be a good rational animal.[53] Being a good K involves the achievement of one's design functions. Hence, achieving one's design functions cannot conflict with one's ideal goals, contrary to what Thomson claims.[54]

The conflict between my account and Thomson's is, thus, not merely apparent. Nevertheless, it may be that a bit of tweaking can reconcile the two views while leaving both relatively the same. For example, Thomson could argue that it is among one's design functions to be a good human, and that this design function is necessarily among one's ideal goals. That is, there is an ideal goal every human has simply in virtue of being human. While this seems to me to result in reconciliation, it may cost Thomson far too much.

Thomson's account of design functions, at least for animate objects, is the familiar etiological theory. Thomson articulates this theory with reference to plants.

> Where Y is a plant, Y is designed to A if it was designed by nature to A. That is so if Y has some features F because possession of F by Y's ancestors increased the likelihood that they would A, where increasing the likelihood that they would A conduced to their reproductive success.[55]

Although Thomson is not explicit, she clearly thinks that the etiological theory is sufficient for explaining the function of humans as well. Given her reliance on the etiological account of function, it seems as though Thomson cannot, after all, accept my proposed emendation. To accept it would require her to say that evolution designed humans in such a way that being a good human was among their functions. As far as I know, no evolutionary story would dare say such a thing with perhaps the chief reason being that to do so would amount to basing selection for traits (at least for humans) on the good of the individual or species.[56] Making selection for traits based on the good of the individual or species undercuts one of the main motivations for etiological accounts, which is to offer a theory of proper function that is value-free.

The reconciliation works only if Thomson expands her notion of human nature and human function in such a way as to include being a good human as a necessary ideal goal of all humans. But to allow this, Thomson must give up the etiological account as it is standardly conceived. Are there independent reasons for Thomson to give up the etiological account? In the next chapter I argue that there are.

CHAPTER 4

THE FUNCTION OF "GOOD" AND GOOD FUNCTIONS

Throughout the last chapter I relied on the notion of a function without explicitly explaining what it is. In this chapter I argue for a normative account of functions. We also saw that J. J. Thomson's account of what is good for a human conflicts with the account I defend. Thomson's account of what is good for a human is divorced from the function of a human. I located the root of the disagreement in our differing conceptions of the nature of functions and the nature of humans. Thomson's account relies on an etiological theory of functions, while my account is either incompatible with etiological accounts or requires a more substantial conception of the nature of humans. Either way, an account of functions is required to more fully explain the kind of moral realism I am advocating. According to the version of moral realism I advocate, the nature and function of humans grounds morality. For ease of exposition, I will hereafter call my account of moral realism Teleological Moral Realism or TMR.

TMR presupposes a theory of functions. Yet, some theories of functions appear to be incompatible with TMR (e.g. Thompson's). Theories of functions fall into three categories: etiological, statistical, and normative.[1] I will argue that the best account of the metaphysics of functions is a normative one that distinguishes between system and part functions, and that this account of functions supports TMR.

1 Etiological and Statistical Theories of Function

Etiological theories, which claim that F is the function of x when x exists because of its tendency to F, and statistical accounts of functions, which claim that F is the function of x when x belongs to a kind whose members normally (understood statistically) F, are incompatible with teleological moral realism.[2] Etiological accounts are incompatible with TMR because they rely too heavily on evolutionary theory. Such reliance rules out the possibility of constructing a moral theory based on the nature and function of humans because the primary function of a kind will be to survive and reproduce (or to facilitate members of the kind to survive and reproduce). If all there is to the function of a human is survival and reproduction, then ethics cannot be derived or built upon the function of a human.[3]

Statistical accounts of functions are incompatible with TMR because an ethical system built upon them would be a version of moral relativism, not moral realism. Relativism follows from a statistical account because the function F of x or kind K changes as soon as a majority of the members of K are no longer F. So F could be the function of humans at t and F^* could be their function at t^*. Since the function of humans would change from t to t^*, what is morally right or good would change as well.[4]

Fortunately for TMR, etiological and statistical theories of functions are false, or so I will argue. In this chapter, I will first explain and refute statistical normality accounts of functions. Second, I will explain and refute etiological accounts of functions. Third, I will explain and defend a normative account of functions. My defense requires slightly modifying the normative account. Lastly, I will argue that a normative account of functions provides both support for TMR and plausible responses to alleged counterexamples to the claim that something is good if, and only if, it is fulfilling its function to such-and-such a degree.

1.1 Statistical Theories of Functions

According to statistical normality theories of functions (SNF), a function is analyzed in terms of statistical normality. Thus, F is the function of x just in case the members of the kind to which x belongs normally Fs. For example, pumping blood is the function of a heart since the kind to which the heart belongs—namely, the heart kind—normally pumps blood. The "normally" in the analysandum is to be understood in a statistical sense. So a more perspicuous way of rendering SNF is the following:

> SNF: F is the function of x iff x is a member of some kind K such that the majority of K's actually F.

SNF gains some plausibility from the fact that it is difficult to see how someone might defend the claim that F is the function of x and x belongs to a kind K that never Fs. Claiming that the function of trees is mobility seems absurd because no tree is mobile and none that we know of ever has been mobile. So, despite the significant problems that beset the SNF account, one can find some intuitive support for the view.

1.2 Objections to SNF

One can mount two kinds of attack on SNF: indirect and direct. The latter kind can be divided into those that deny the necessary condition and those that deny the sufficient condition. We will begin with these and then turn to three indirect objections to SNF.

1.3 Against the Necessary Condition of SNF

The necessary condition, according to SNF, for F being the function of x is that x belongs to a K such that the majority of K's actually F. Michael Rea, drawing on some of Plantinga's criticisms, argues that it is possible for F to be the function of x despite the fact that x belongs to a K such that the majority of the Ks do not actually F.[5] Consider, for example, the function of the optic nerve. Its function is to transmit information to the visual cortex. If this became abnormal, if the majority of optic nerves no longer did transmit information, clearly, transmitting information to the visual cortex would not cease to be the optic nerve's proper function.[6] It is not necessary for F to be the function of x that a majority of xs F. Another example is that of sperm. The function of sperm is to fertilize an egg. But since very few sperm manage to achieve this result, SNF implies that egg fertilization cannot be the sperm's function. Yet clearly sperm do have this function.

1.4 Against the Sufficient Condition of SNF

The sufficient condition of SNF is also problematic. According to it, if a majority of xs belonging to K F, then F is the function of x. The major difficulty is that the antecedent does not distinguish between a thing's function and its accidental properties. Consider once again the heart. The majority of hearts make a thumping sound. But making a thumping sound is not the function of the heart. By failing to distinguish between a thing's function and its accidental properties SNF implausibly attributes far too many functions to at least some things. Since the majority of hearts make a thumping sound, according to SNF hearts have the function of making a thumping sound. But obviously making a thumping sound is not the function of a heart. Hence, SNF is false.[7]

SNF also cannot adequately explain malfunction. If all of the xs F, then F is the function of x. Now imagine, as we did for the optic nerve, that the majority of hearts stop pumping blood. It would seem that the correct thing to say is that the majority of hearts are malfunctioning. But the SNF advocate cannot say that the majority of hearts are malfunctioning. SNF is false.[8]

1.5 Indirect Objections to SNF

Our first indirect objection highlights the connection between fulfilling one's function and being a good member of one's kind. SNF implies that fulfilling the function of x is neither a necessary nor sufficient condition for x being a good K. But fulfilling the function of x is necessary (and may be sufficient in some cases) for x being a good K. Hence, SNF is false.[9]

If F is the function of x, then the majority of xs F, according to SNF. That the majority of xs F is a necessary condition for F being the function of x. But if SNF is true, x could be a good instance of its kind but nevertheless not perform F even though the majority of xs, *ex hypothesi*, do. Consider again Rea's example of the optic nerve. A good optic nerve is one that transmits information to the visual cortex. Imagine that the majority of optic nerves fail to transmit information. Then, SNF would judge that a lone optic nerve that still transmits information to the visual cortex functions rather poorly even though that lone optic nerve is a good one. But this is false. A thing cannot be a good instance of its kind and function poorly at the same time.

Or assume, for the sake of argument, that making a thumping sound is the function of hearts. A heart, however, could be a bad heart and still make a thumping sound. Thus, SNF wrongly implies that something can be a fully functioning member of its kind and yet not be a good instance of its kind.[10]

According to the second indirect objection, SNF fails because it uses the actual behavior of members of a kind to analyze functions. In other words, SNF does not provide a metaphysical account of function, but an account of function that, if true (and we have seen that there are good reasons to think that it is not true), is indexed to the actual world only. This is a serious objection, because in other worlds SNF may have no application, and yet these other worlds could have entities that have functions.[11]

The third indirect objection comes from the connection between natures and functions spelled out in Chapter 3. Given the essential connection between natures and functions, if the function of Ks changes, then Ks go out of existence since the primary function of a member of a kind is essential to it. On SNF, a thing can change its function because of a change in activity of other members of its kind. For example, suppose the function of hearts is to pump blood because this is what the majority of hearts actually do. If over time or simultaneously the majority of hearts no longer pumped blood, then the function of hearts would change. Now consider some heart that continues to pump blood. That heart's function has also changed. Thus, if it continues to pump blood when the others hearts have stopped it is no longer a heart. This implication makes the nature of a thing completely extrinsic. But natures are not extrinsic is such a radical way.[12] I continue to be a human no matter what my peers do and hearts continue to be hearts no matter what their "peers" do.[13]

1.6 Etiological Theories of Functions

Since Ruth Millikan's etiological theory of functions is by far the most developed account, I will focus on her version.[14] It is important to note at the outset that etiological accounts do not commit the same mistakes that SNF does. Millikan claims that "It is not then the actual constitution, powers, or dispositions of a thing that make it a member of a certain biological category."[15] The biological category of heart and the connection that this category has with pumping blood must be specified more precisely than simply to note that hearts pump blood. Some hearts cannot pump blood, and some things that are not hearts can pump blood. Hence, pumping blood cannot be what distinguishes hearts from non-hearts. According to etiological accounts, a thing's proper function places it in its biological category, and the proper function of a thing has to do with its history, not its powers.[16] By focusing on history, Millikan seeks to define proper function using naturalistic, non-normative terms.

While the details of Millikan's account are given in *Language, Thought, and Other Biological Categories,* Millikan provides a much more manageable description of proper function in her article "In Defense of Proper Functions." There she writes:

> The definition of "proper function" is recursive. Putting things very roughly, for an item A to have a function F as a "proper function," it is necessary (and close to sufficient) that one of these two conditions should hold. (1) A originated as a "reproduction" (to give one example, as a copy, or a copy of a copy) of some prior item or items that, *due* in part to possession of the properties reproduced, have actually performed F in the past, and A exists because (causally historically because) of this or these performances. (2) A originated as the product of some prior device that, given its circumstances, had performance of F as a proper function and that, under those circumstances, normally causes F to be performed by *means* of producing an item like A. Items that fall under condition (2) have "derived proper functions," functions derived from the functions of the devices that produce them.[17]

Millikan's account is meant to stress the historical. An object's or kind's function is determined in part by what its ancestors did. Thus, when characterizing Millikan's etiological account it is important to include the historical condition. For brevity, the following summary of Millikan's account will suffice:

> *Etiological Account* (EA): x has F as its function iff x exists because of its tendency to F and x has a tendency to F because x's ancestors Fed.[18]

The connection between Millikan's account and evolutionary theory should be clear. Hearts have the function of pumping blood because their tendency to pump blood helps to explain their existence, and the tendency to pump blood is present in the first place because ancestor hearts pumped blood. Pumping blood was selected for in hearts because it is conducive to survival and reproductive success.

1.7 Objections to EA

Like direct objections to SNF, direct objections to EA challenge either the necessary or the sufficient condition. And again, like SNF, EA faces a couple of indirect objections.

1.8 Against the Necessary Condition of EA

EA appeals to a thing's reproductive history as a necessary condition in order to specify what the thing's proper function(s) is (are). If the proper function of x is F, then F must figure into the reproductive history of x in such a way that the presence of F contributes to the survival and fitness of x. Alternatively, if F does not figure into the reproductive history of x, then F cannot be the proper function of x. So to generate a counter-example to EA's necessary condition, one must show that it is possible for F to be the function of x despite the fact that F does not figure into its reproductive history.

According to Alvin Plantinga, "A thing need not have *ancestors* to have a proper function. . . ."[19] Plantinga notes that this seems to be so in both natural and conscious (artifact) cases. With respect to the latter, he points out that the first telephone could have had a proper function. If it is possible that the first telephone had a proper function, then EA is false.

Recall Millikan's first necessary condition for an item A to have F as a proper function. "A originated as a "reproduction" (to give one example, as a copy, or a copy of a copy) of some prior item or items that, *due* in part to possession of the properties reproduced, have actually performed F in the past, and A exists because (causally historically because) of this or these performances." In Plantinga's example, the first telephone is clearly not a reproduction of some prior item. The very possibility of a first artifact with a proper function seems to suggest that Millikan's necessary condition is not necessary after all. That is, it is possible for something to have a proper function without having ancestors and, a fortiori, without having ancestors that actually performed the function.

With respect to natural cases, Plantinga points out that God could have created Adam and Eve instantaneously. Hence, Adam's heart would have had a proper function even though his heart had no ancestors. Plantinga concludes that the ancestral condition in etiological accounts is not necessary.

1.9 Against the Sufficient Condition of EA

According to EA, if x exists because of its tendency to F and x has a tendency to F because x's ancestors Fed, then x has F as its proper function. Michael Rea argues that there is no important connection between reproductive history and proper function since the two can diverge. Imagine that S is an incompetent demigod. S designs x intending x to F; x evolves and does not F. Instead, x non-Fs. That x non-Fs and that non-Fing is a part of x's reproductive history do not mean that non-Fing is x's proper function.

Reproductive clay crystals provide another sort of counterexample to the sufficient condition of EA. Damming up streams is something that clay crystals do, and damming up streams is involved in their reproductive history. So, according to EA, damming up streams is the proper function of clay crystals. But "no one would want to say that there is any metaphysically important sense in which the crystals are *supposed* to dam up streams."[20]

Plantinga raises a different objection to the sufficient condition. Imagine that Hitler's scientists introduce a mutation in the visual system of non-Aryans. The mutation is such that for those who have it, life is awful. Hitler also begins to wipe out any non-Aryan without the mutation. The mutation spreads and "the number of non-mutants dwindles. But then consider some nth generation mutant m."[21] This member's visual system will meet all of the purported sufficient conditions for having a proper function, but surely we do not want to say that m's visual system is functioning properly. It is possible to satisfy EA's sufficient condition for having a proper function without having a proper function. Hence, EA is false.

1.10 Indirect Objections

One indirect objection Rea raises works against both EA and SNF and comes in two parts. Notice that according to both EA and SNF, x has a proper function just in case it bears some relation to something other than itself. For SNF, x must bear some relation to other members of the kind to which x belongs in order for x to have a proper function. For EA, x must bear some relation to x's ancestors in order for x to have a proper function. Hence, according to both EA and SNF, "biological organisms cannot exist alone- they can only exist in groups."[22] Given that biological organisms cannot exist alone, it follows that there was not a first cell.[23]

0. There was a first cell.
1. If a cell exists, it has modal properties.[24]
2. If a cell has modal properties, it has proper functions.[25]
3. If a cell has proper functions, then there are other cells.[26]
4. Therefore, there was no first cell.

EA and SNF appear to imply that there was no first cell or indeed no first member in any series with a function.

Robert Koons and many others have also noted that EA implies members of a kind with function F cannot have a first member with F as its function.[27] This appears to follow straightforwardly from EA. Functions are derived from ancestors. In order to stop an infinite regress of ancestors with function F, there must be a first member in the series that does not have the relevant function. If the first member in the series does have F as its function, then EA is false, since there are no ancestors. Granting that EA implies the first members in a series cannot have the function that the other members in the series have seems to many philosophers to be a serious objection to EA. I am not so sure.

To stop an infinite regress, EA advocates must claim that in any series where members have function F, first members cannot have F as their function. But, we may ask, first members of what? Consider the heart kind. Hearts have the function of pumping blood, and hearts have this function, in part, because of their history. At some point in the history of the heart, some ancestor A began to pump blood without pumping blood being A's function. But according to EA, kinds are distinguished by their functions. In order for A to be a member of the heart kind, A must have the function of a heart. *Ex hypothesi* A does not have the function of a heart. Thus, A is not a heart.

The first member objection (we may call it) seems to assume that the first member in the series of things having F for their function must have F for its function. But this just seems to beg the question against EA. The first member is not a member of, for example, the heart kind since it does not have as its function what hearts have as their function. Rather, the first member in the series of things with F as their function is merely a member of the class of things that has F as a property. The first item that begins to pump blood in an organism does not have pumping blood as its function, but nevertheless has being able to pump blood as one of its properties. The first member passes on to its progeny the property of being able to pump blood, and the progeny (via natural selection) gain the property of being able to pump blood as their proper function. As it stands, the first member objection appears to fail. However, there may be a way to repair it so that it is even more damaging to EA than its original formulation.

Consider again the etiological account. x has F as its proper function iff x exists because of its tendency to F and x has a tendency to F because x's ancestors Fed. For EA, inclusion into a biological category depends on a thing's proper function. If x's proper function is F and F is necessary and sufficient for being a member of biological category B, then x is a member of B. If x loses F as its proper function, then x is no longer a member of B. Now, it is plausible that being a member of a biological category is an essential property of anything that has the property. Being a member of B is essential to x.

According to EA (and simplifying a bit), x has proper function F only if x's ancestors performed F. But if F is the proper function of x, then x is a member of biological category B. So if x's ancestors had F as their proper function, x's ancestors are members of B. Now assume that x's ancestors have F as their proper function only if their ancestors had F as their proper function. Again, F is sufficient for inclusion in B. The ancestors of the ancestors are members of B. Repetitive application results in the following dilemma: either the biological category B always had members, in which case Darwinism is false, or there was a time t such that at t some ancestor A of x (where x has F as its proper function) performed F but at t A's performance of F was not A's proper function. If the first disjunct is adopted, then contrary to the proponents of etiological theories, etiological theories actually entail the *falsity* of Darwinism. EA theorists must grasp the second disjunct. But the second disjunct has a serious problem.

EA theorists must, it seems, accept the following: there was a time t such that at t some ancestor A of x (where x has F as its proper function) performed F but at t A's performance of F was not A's proper function. Given that having F as a proper function is sufficient for inclusion in biological category B, EA advocates would also appear to be committed to the following: for all x, y, if x has property F and F is the proper function of y, then it is possible that F is not the proper function of x. In the artifactual case, this is clearly true. My book has the property of being used as a doorstop, whereas the doorstop I just purchased has the proper function of being a doorstop. It is possible for x to have the property F, y to have F as its proper function and x not to have F as its proper function.

In the biological case, it is not as obvious that x can have a property F such that when F is the function of y, F is sufficient for inclusion in biological category B, but merely having F is not sufficient for inclusion in B. Consider a human. If x is a human, it is plausible to suppose that being human is x's most fundamental kind.[28] Furthermore, it seems plausible that if anything has the property being human, it essentially is a human. That is, in the biological case (or at least some instances of the biological case), it is necessary that if x has property H and H is the most fundamental kind for y, then H is the most fundamental kind for x. If the principle is true, then EA is in serious trouble. Indeed, even if it is the case that the principle is false but there is *one* instance in the biological realm where possessing a property that is fundamental for x implies possessing it is fundamental for anything that has it, EA is in serious trouble. The principle implies that for at least some biological cases it is not possible for x to pass on a property to y that is essential to y but not to x. For example, it is impossible for something that is a non-human to pass on the property of being human[29] because whatever has the property of being human is essentially human.[30]

Robert Koons raises a second indirect objection to EA. Koons notes that EA advocates have busied themselves attempting either to refine the account in order to escape the first member objection (e.g. prospective accounts that are forward looking) or by biting the bullet and arguing that the benefits of the account outweigh the costs. Koons goes on to note that "[t]here is, however, a more fundamental problem with all of these accounts: the fact that they make the truth of Darwinism a matter of ontological necessity."[31] In a world where Darwinism is false, the individuals in that world do not have functions, according to EA. But this seems implausible (to say the least). If we go on to discover that Darwinism is false, we would not conclude that hearts and language and optic nerves do not have functions.

Plantinga raises the same objection. According to him, since evolutionary theory is, at best, contingently true, no account of proper function can presuppose the truth of evolutionary theory. If an account of proper function presupposes the truth of evolutionary theory, then the account would only be contingently true. But if evolutionary theory turns out false, which it could, then our account of proper function would also be false. Things would still have functions, just not functions that are to be explained in terms of evolutionary theory.[32]

Etiological accounts of function fail on several levels. As such, any theory of morality that attempts to use functions as part of its base must avoid being committed to EA. Given that both SNF and EA are false, we must look elsewhere for a theory of functions upon which to ground morality. In my estimation, Robert Koons's normative theory is the best place to look.

2 Normative Theories of Functions

I argue that something like a normative account of functions, supplemented with a distinction between system and part functions, is correct—where normative accounts can explain the fact that if F is the function of x, then x is *supposed* to F. A normative theory of functions is not only compatible with TMR, it supports TMR.[33]

According to Koons, "[a] thing is capable of well-being just in case the sum of its Wright-functions forms a highly coherent, mutually supportive totality."[34] A thing has a Wright-function just in case "the fact that things in kind v have state φ is causally explained (at least in part) by the existence of a causal law linking (φ & v) to ψ as cause to effect."[35] The Wright-function by itself will not succeed in capturing what a function is, since it too falls prey to some of the objections canvassed above. For example, Plantinga's objection to the sufficient condition of etiological accounts is applicable to Wright-functions. The members of v have a state—a mutation in their visual system—that is causally explained by the existence of a causal law linking the visual system and the members of a kind to ψ as cause to effect. But by adding that the Wright-functions form a "highly coherent, mutually supportive totality" Koons thus sidesteps Plantinga's objection.

Koons goes on to claim that a thing has a good iff it has proper functions.[36] The good of a thing consists in the successful exercise of its primary proper functions. Primary proper functions are distinguished from secondary proper functions in that the latter are operative only when the former malfunction or fail.[37] Furthermore, accidental satisfaction of well-being is distinguished from non-accidental satisfaction of well-being in that the latter but not the former is explained by a thing's aiming toward a sum of Wright-functions that forms a highly coherent, mutually supportive totality. In other words, since it is possible for some things to have the sum of Wright functions to form a highly coherent, mutually supportive totality without there being any functional organization, we need to be able to distinguish between cases where there is functional organization from cases where there is not. For example, ice in a rock crevice causes the crevice to remain open, and the existence of the ice in the crevice is caused by its power to keep the crevice open.[38] There seems to be a highly coherent, mutually supportive totality here, and yet we would not attribute functionality to the ice. It is not the ice's function to keep the crevice open.

Koons is able to separate the accidental satisfaction from the non-accidental satisfaction of well-being by adding an additional clause. If the existence of the thing is caused (in part) by the highly coherent, mutually supportive totality plus Koons's other conditions, then the thing has a proper function. From these considerations, Koons's develops the following account of proper function:

2.1 Aristotelian Definition of Proper Function

A state φ has the proper function ψ in kind v if and only if:

1. The fact that things in kind v have state φ is causally explained (at least in part) by a causal law linking (φ & v) to ψ as cause to effect (Wright's condition).
2. The system of functions $<\varphi_i, \psi_i>$ meeting condition (1) for v forms a mostly harmonious, mutually supportive whole, and the $<\varphi, \psi>$ function contributes to this harmony.
3. The existence of things of kind v is causally explained (at least in part) by the harmony mentioned in condition (2).

Koons goes on to explain the notion of harmony at work in the second and third conditions. Koons writes:

> Let us say that function x harmonizes with system S just in case
> 1. for many, but not necessarily all, members y of S, the fulfillment of x increases the probability of the fulfillment of y.
> 2. for most but not necessarily all members y of S, the fulfillment of x does not significantly decrease the probability of the fulfillment of y.

The ice in the rock crevice fails to meet the third condition. While it is plausible to suppose that the ice in the rock crevice keeps the rock crevice open and that the opening in the crevice keeps the ice where it is because of some causal law (first condition) and that the crevice and the ice form a mostly harmonious, mutually supportive whole, the fact that neither the existence of the ice nor the crevice remaining open is causally explained by the mostly harmonious, mutually supportive whole shows that it is false, according to Koons's criteria, to attribute a proper function either to the ice or the crevice. Failure to meet the third condition is sufficient to show that there is no proper function. As we shall see, critics of Koons's account sometimes fail to appreciate the force of the third condition.

Before moving on to discuss some objections to Koons's account, it is important to note the implicit connection between natures and functions that is at work in the above definitions. Koons explains that a function harmonizes within a system if, and only if, the function increases the probability of the system's fulfillment and does not decrease the probability of the fulfillment of the system. The kind of system is clearly relevant. In some systems, fulfilling the function of x would increase the probability of the system's fulfillment (where fulfillment of the system is understood in terms of fulfillment of the things' primary functions), whereas, in other systems, fulfillment of x would not increase the fulfillment of the system and might decrease the fulfillment of the system. Lubricating one's lawnmower with oil helps to increase the lawnmower's fulfillment of its primary functions, whereas lubricating one's stomach with oil would not. The nature of a thing will determine to a large extent the nature of the functions that harmonize within it. As Christopher Megone notes while explaining and defending an Aristotelian or normative account of function, "... it is not possible to understand the sense in which illness is a failure of function without grasping the way in which certain changes contribute to a good human life as a whole. Functional explanation only makes sense in the light of the function of the whole."[39] In order to claim that part of a system is malfunctioning, one must have some idea of the function of the whole system. Koons's account helps us determine what the function of the whole system is by implicitly drawing our attention to the nature of the thing and emphasizing its primary functions.

There are some difficulties for Koons's account. By considering the difficulties we will both be able to better understand some of the details of his position and see what needs to be added to stave off counter-examples.

2.2 Objections to Normative Accounts of Function

Michael Rea summarizes Koons's account thusly: "The proper function of a thing in a system is to perform whichever of its functions appropriately contributes to the well-being or flourishing of the system."[40] Rea goes on to argue that Koons's account appears to make the damming up of streams a proper function of clay crystals.

> Imagine a kind of clay that improves its own chance of being deposited by damming up streams. The streams form shallow pools which then dry up. The clay dries and is blown away as dust, only to be deposited in other streams. The new crystals reproduce themselves and dam up their respective streams.[41]

Rea claims that "no one would want to say that there is any metaphysically important sense in which the crystals are *supposed* to dam up streams."[42]

The phenomena described above seem to satisfy the first condition of Koons's definition of proper function. "These crystals exist where they are in part because they dam up streams."[43] What about Koons's second condition? According to Rea this condition is also satisfied if we imagine that clay crystals are part of a larger system (the ecosystem) such that the existence of clay crystals contributes to the flourishing of this larger system. Interestingly, Rea is silent on whether Koons's third condition is met. To meet the third condition, Rea must say it is possible that clay crystals exist, in part, because they contribute to the flourishing of this larger system. But notice that once we add this third condition—that is, if we grant that clay crystals exist because they contribute to the flourishing of the ecosystem—it *does* seem as though clay crystals' proper function is to dam up streams. After all, that is why clay crystals exist (granting that the third condition is met), and their existence does indeed contribute to the flourishing of the system of which they are parts.

If the third condition is not met—that is, if we deny that clay crystals exist because they contribute to the flourishing of the ecosystem—then the clay crystal example is not a counter-example. If the third condition is met, then it is far from obvious that "no one would want to say that there is any metaphysically important sense in which the crystals are *supposed* to dam up streams." The crystals exist (granting that the third condition is met) in part because they dam up streams. That seems metaphysically important. I conclude that Rea's first objection fails either because it does not meet the conditions Koons's specifies or because when an expanded example satisfies all of Koons's conditions the objection loses considerable force.

Another way to see the failure of Rea's objection is by considering another of his examples in which he articulates an important distinction. First, the example that Rea believes undermines Koons' account.

> [L]ower organisms in a food chain are plausibly thought to owe their existence in part to the fact that they themselves serve as food for organisms higher in the chain. For example, zooplankton feed on phytoplankton and, in turn, serve as food for larger fish which are ultimately converted into nutrients that support zooplankton. Thus, there is a clear sense in which zooplankton owe their existence in a marine ecosystem in part to the fact that they serve as food for larger fish. Thus, zooplankton apparently have the Wright-function of feeding larger fish. Furthermore, it is quite plausible to think that this Wright-function is a contributing member of a mutually supportive harmonious system of similar Wright-functions performed by other parts of the same ecosystem, and that the relevant harmony partly causally explains the existence of ecosystems of that sort. But then it follows that zooplankton have as their proper function the property of being food for higher organisms.[44]

This is supposed to present a problem for Koons because Koons's account appears to require that proper functions somehow contribute to flourishing.[45] But if the proper function of zooplankton is to be food for higher organisms, then the proper function of zooplankton does not contribute to zooplankton's flourishing. Indeed, it would seem as if the proper function of zooplankton is deleterious to zooplankton. What is needed is a distinction between the proper function of zooplankton qua zooplankton and the proper function of zooplankton qua members of an ecosystem. Rea himself provides such a distinction.

Rea distinguishes between proper system and proper part functions. The proper system function for some organism is simply that organism's proper function considered without reference to some larger system of which the organism is a part. For example, the proper system function of a cat may be something like being healthy. The proper part function of a thing depends on the contribution that the thing makes to the overall system of which it is a part.[46] With the distinction between proper system and proper part function in mind, we are now in a position to see just where Rea's objection goes wrong.

Rea suggests that when considering proper system functions (e.g. the proper function of zooplankton qua zooplankton) we are considering whether the thing is healthy—or something analogous to health in the case of artifacts (e.g. the proper function of the thing's primary functions). So, a healthy zooplankton will not be one that has been used for food by some higher organism. But the fact that the proper system function of zooplankton is not to be used for food by some higher organism is compatible with saying that the proper part function of zooplankton is being food for higher organisms. A healthy ecosystem may require something bad for some of its parts. This is not surprising. In Chapter 2 I argued that the following is true:

> *Good to Bad Kind-Interaction*: A good member of some kind K may enter into relations with some other kind K* and some of the relations that K enters into with K* may be bad for members of K* or bad for members of K.

The case we are now considering is such that one of the parts of the ecosystem has a proper system function that cannot be preserved if the ecosystem is to fulfill its proper function. In other words, the fulfillment of K's proper functions may be deleterious to the fulfillment of the proper functions of K*. There is nothing at all counter-intuitive about such an arrangement.

The problem with Rea's objection is that it equivocates on two different notions of proper function—the very notions that Rea himself highlights. When Rea claims that Koons's account of proper function implies that the proper function of zooplankton is being food for higher organisms, Rea assumes that most readers will find this consequence absurd. But given the distinction between proper part functions and proper system functions, the objection loses much (if not all) of its force. Koons's account does not imply that the proper system function of zooplankton is to be food for higher animals.

Rea's final objection to Koons's account is, in my opinion, the most pressing.

> [C]onsider an artifact whose overall design plan includes a self-destruct mechanism. Plausibly, a self-destruct mechanism is supposed to destroy the artifact of which it is a part—that is its proper function. But except in contrived cases, self-destruct mechanisms make no contribution whatsoever to the overall well-being of the things of which they are parts. Thus, even if Koons's definition does provide a sufficient condition for having a proper function, it does not provide a necessary condition.[47]

In other words, the proper function of the mechanism is to destroy the artifact. But destroying the artifact does not contribute to the "well-being" of the artifact. It is possible for something to have a proper function that does not contribute to the well-being of the system of which it is a part.

We need to present the objection a bit more clearly, and in the process we will see that the objection fails. There are at least two different ways of understanding Rea's worry. The first way involves a diachronic reading of the self-destruct objection (as we may call it). The second way is a synchronic reading.

According to the diachronic reading of the self-destruct objection, the artifact has some function F that it can successfully perform only if, once performed, the self-destruct mechanism performs its function and destroys the artifact. In other words, the artifact has a proper function and is capable of performing this proper function without interference from the self-destruct mechanism. The self-destruct mechanism begins to operate after the artifact has successfully performed its function. It does not appear that this way of understanding the objection poses any problem to the normative account of functions under consideration.[48]

The artifact achieves the analogue of well-being when it successfully performs its proper function. Each of its parts, other than the self-destruct mechanism, we may assume, contributes in some way to the artifact's performance of its proper function. Contribution to well-being plays a vital role in the artifact's performance of its proper function. The fact that the self-destruct mechanism functions properly only after the artifact has successfully performed its proper function does not seem to show that the self-destruct mechanism's proper function inhibits the proper function of the artifact or the artifact's well-being in any way.

According to the synchronic reading of the self-destruct objection, the artifact has some function F that it can perform only if the self-destruct mechanism simultaneously performs its proper function. There are two types of cases we can consider under the synchronic reading of the self-destruct objection. The first case states that the function of the artifact is different from the function of the self-destruct mechanism, while the second case assumes that the function of the artifact is the same as the function of the self-destruct mechanism. I will argue that neither case shows that the normative theory of functions fails.

The first case under the synchronic reading of the self-destruct objection states that the function of the artifact is different from the function of the self-destruct mechanism. If we assume that the artifact's proper function is different from the proper function of the self-destruct mechanism, then if it is possible for the artifact to perform its function, it must be possible that the artifact performs its function simultaneously with the successful performance of the self-destruct mechanism's function.[49] For example, imagine an artifact with three parts and assume that the artifact does not come into existence until all of the parts are properly arranged. Once the parts are properly arranged, the artifact simultaneously sprays water and destroys itself, just as the designer intended. The artifact appears to function precisely as it is supposed to.

According to the second case of the synchronic reading of the self-destruct objection, the artifact has some function that it can perform only if the self-destruct mechanism simultaneously performs its proper function. In this second case, we are to assume that the artifact's proper function is the same as the proper function of the self-destruct mechanism. The proper function of the artifact is self-destruction. For example, imagine an artifact with three parts and assume that the artifact does not come into existence until all of the parts are properly arranged. Once the parts are properly arranged, the artifact immediately destroys itself, just as the designer intended. The artifact appears to function precisely as it is supposed to.

The two different versions of the synchronic reading of the self-destruct objection do pose a challenge to normative theories of function. Nevertheless, the challenge can be met. In the case of an artifact it is plausible to suppose (as we did in Chapter 3) that the nature of the artifact is determined by its function. Furthermore, the function of the artifact is determined by the intentions of the designer. Assuming with Rea that the designer intended the artifact to self-destruct, it follows that the function of the artifact is to self-destruct. Presumably, making an artifact that self-destructs is viewed by the designer as some kind of good.[50] Perhaps the designer enjoys seeing things self-destruct. Perhaps the designer intends the artifact to deliver a message, and once it is received, the artifact self-destructs (this is the diachronic case considered above). What is important to realize is that artifacts cannot exist without intentions. In a world without intenders, there cannot be any artifacts. What this shows is that it is misleading to consider the function of an artifact apart from the intentions of the designer. If the designer intends an artifact to F, then the designer believes that performances of F in circumstances C are good for someone or something. But the relevance of intentions to the nature of artifacts implies that the well-being of an artifact is determined not simply by the artifact considered in isolation, but rather by the artifact considered as part of a system where intentions are a significant part. If it turns out that the intentions of the designer decrease the well-being of the designer or decrease the well-being of others, then, given that a person intends to A only if a person believes that A contributes to his or her well-being or the well-being of his or her community, it follows that the intention fails to perform its proper function. The function of the artifact is dependent on an intention, and intentions can fail to perform their function of contributing to the well-being of the intender or the intender's community.

Here is an example of what I have in mind. Suppose Steve intends to make a device that kills all and only dentists. The device performs its function quite well. Hence, we might say the device is properly functioning. But Steve's intention can be evaluated as well.[51] Does Steve's intention contribute to the over-all well-being of Steve or of Steve's community? Clearly, it does not. Even if the device never manages to perform its proper function, the very fact of its having the proper function it has is dependent on an intention that is deleterious to both the intender and the community. Given that one of the functions of intentions is to contribute to the well-being of the intender (or others in the community), it follows that the intention to kill all and only dentists malfunctions.

The intention to kill all and only dentists does not fulfill an intention's function of contributing to the well-being of the intender. So, in one sense the device can function properly and in another sense the device cannot.

The device functions properly just in case it fulfills the intentions of the designer. The device fails to function properly just in case it does not fulfill the intentions of the designer.[52] In the case we are imagining, the designer actually has two intentions. One is a sort of meta-intention: intend all and only those things that contribute to the well-being of myself or my community. The other is a first-order intention: make a device that kills all and only dentists. At the first-order level, the device performs its proper function just in case it succeeds in killing all and only dentists (and does so non-accidentally). At the meta-level, the device fails to perform its function since its function fails to contribute to the well-being of the designer and the community. My suggestion is that by failing to recognize this distinction Rea's objection fails.

We cannot specify the proper function of the artifact that has a self-destruct mechanism as a part without knowing the intentions of the designer. Assuming the artifact in question does contribute to the well-being of the designer, then the artifact performs its proper function and fulfilling its proper function is good for the designer. The artifact fulfills both the first-order intentions and the meta-level intentions of the designer. As such, the artifact has fulfilled its proper function, and its proper function does, contrary to Rea, contribute to the overall well-being of the system of which the device is a part. Rea simply focuses on the wrong system.

Assume that the artifact in question does not contribute to the well-being of the designer. In this case, the artifact fails to perform its meta-level proper function. Since it fails to perform its meta-level proper function the artifact malfunctions. The fact that the artifact malfunctions at even one level, the meta-level, is sufficient for the artifact to malfunction. That is, in order for the artifact to function properly it must function properly at both the first-order level and the meta-level. Rea's objection works only if we assume that the function of the artifact is exhausted by the first-order intentions of the designer. But I see no good reason to assume this. Hence, Rea's final and most pressing objection fails.

3 Answering Objections to TMR with the Normative Theory of Functions

Now that we have an account of function that is both free from the defects affecting other accounts and clearly supports the version of moral realism defended here, I am in a position to respond to perhaps the most common and seemingly difficult objections to TMR. The attributive account of "good" implies that only things with functions or natures are good. This implication is considered by many to be a *reductio* of the attributive account, for things without functions can be good. Hence, the attributive account must be wrong. Yet, a normative theory of functions together with a distinction between system and part functions provides TMR with a plausible response to this objection.

The claim that things without functions can be good is ambiguous between the following three claims: (a) things without system functions can be good; (b) things without part functions can be good; and (c) things lacking both system and part functions can be good. I argue that only (c) spells trouble for TMR and that (c) is false.

In Chapters 2 and 3, I argued that the claim "x is good" is elliptical for "x is a good K." I went on to argue that this implies that x has a function and that the function of x is determined by its primary kind. The normative account of functions supports the claim that x is a good K iff x has a function. According to the normative account, a thing has a function iff a thing has a good. But now consider the claim (assume that it is true) that this rock is good. According to TMR, this claim implies that this rock is a good K and that the K supplies the rock with its function. But this looks implausible. Rocks simply do not have functions.

Or consider the claim that this particular sunset is good. According to TMR, this claim implies that the sunset is a good K, and the K supplies the sunset with its function. But sunsets do not have functions. Examples can be multiplied, but these two should suffice. These objections to TMR assume that TMR is committed to the following:

If x is good, then x has a proper system function and x is performing its proper system function to such and such a degree.

But TMR is not committed to such a claim. Given the distinction between proper system functions and proper part functions TMR is committed to the following (at most)[53]:

x is good iff:

x has a proper system function and x is performing its proper system function to such and such a degree

Or

x has a proper part function and x is performing its proper part function to such and such a degree.

It is no objection to TMR to say that rocks do not have system functions but that rocks can still be good. Indeed, it is highly unlikely that anyone would ever say of some rock that it has a proper system function. Instead, if someone claims that this is a good rock, she likely means that the rock is good for storing heat or as a doorstop or etc. . . . . But to say that a rock is good because it contributes to something is just to say that the rock is performing is proper part function to such-and-such a degree.

The diagnosis of the objection with respect to rocks will also work with respect to sunsets. First, notice that the claim that this is a good sunset is likely to mean something like "this is a good sunset for viewing" or "this is a good sunset for drawing" or, ... But if these elaborations are correct, then the sunset is good because it contributes to something else. The goodness of the sunset is a function of its contribution to a larger system and thus the sunset has a proper part function.

We can apply the same style of response, *mutatis mutandis*, to claims that deny a proper part function to something while claiming that the thing is good. In these cases it is likely that the thing's function is well-being or some analogue of well-being. The proper part function/proper system function distinction allows TMR to sidestep these common objections in a way that fits the best account of functions we have.

If something does not have a proper part function and does not have a proper system function, then according to TMR that thing cannot be good. I simply cannot think of anything that does not have (or could not have) either kind of function and yet could be good. The reason for the difficulty in coming up with a plausible example is because it will always be possible to rephrase the claim in terms of either proper part function or proper system function. The above rephrases with rocks and sunsets are examples of how to do it.

I want to close by making an observation about the nature of predicate-forming functors or, as we may also call them, property-markers. From the claim that "good" is a predicate-forming functor it does not follow that just anything can be substituted as an argument and a value will result. Consider another predicate-forming functor, "square-of." "Square-of" takes certain objects as arguments and yields certain objects as values. But it is just a mistake to think that it is permissible to put whatever one likes in the argument place. The functor itself determines what the permissible arguments are. The same, it seems, is true of the predicate-forming functor "good." "Good" determines the nature of its arguments, which, when substituted, determine the nature of the value.

In the next chapter I will argue that TMR, with its heavy reliance on the attributive account of "good," implies the convertibility of being and goodness. Anything that has being is good, and anything good has being. That implication may seem to be incompatible with the idea that "good" is a predicate-forming functor that determines the nature of its arguments. But the incompatibility is only apparent, so long as we remember the distinction between proper part and proper system functions. It is possible to substitute anything that has being into the argument place of "good," so long as the whole statement either implicitly or explicitly refers to a thing with either a system or part function.[54]

Chapter 5

From the Attributive Account to God

In this final chapter I will present two additional metaethical consequences of the attributive account. I include these consequences here and not in Chapter 3 because those discussed here have some interesting implications for philosophy of religion. While various issues within the philosophy of religion occupied our attention in Chapter 1, the issues within philosophy of religion discussed in the present chapter will move us beyond the metaethical context. Hence, a separate treatment, and a separate chapter, seemed advisable.

Two consequences of the attributive account will occupy the first two sections of this chapter: the convertibility of being and goodness and the privation theory of evil. Once we have these before us, I will argue that the attributive account provides the starting point for a few different, though related, arguments for God's existence. I will end this chapter and the book by noting some interesting consequences of the attributive account for the problem of evil.

1 From Attributive Account to Convertibility of Being and Goodness

My chief goal in this section is not to defend the idea that being and goodness are identical. Rather, my aim in this section is to defend the claim that the attributive account of "good" implies the convertibility thesis.

In this section I will defend the following:

> *Convertibility Claim* (CC): If "good" is attributive, then the convertibility thesis—that being and goodness are identical—is true.

There are, in general, two ways to defend CC. The first way is direct and simply attempts to demonstrate that the consequent of CC is true given the antecedent (or, put more weakly, that the consequent is probably true, given the antecedent). The second way is indirect and attempts to show that CC is true by showing that the attributive thesis implies the privation theory of evil and that the privation theory of evil implies the convertibility of being and goodness. In this section I attempt the former, direct defense of CC, and in the next section I attempt the latter, indirect defense of CC. The former strikes me as being the more difficult of the two ways of defending CC, and I am not as confident in the arguments of this section as I am in the arguments of the next section.

The consequent of the convertibility claim needs a bit of unpacking. The idea is that the terms "goodness" and "being" are the same in reference and differ only in sense. This seems to be what Aquinas has in mind when, in his defense of the convertibility of being and goodness, he responds to an objection by noting the differences between unqualified being, unqualified goodness, qualified being, and qualified goodness.[1]

According to Aquinas, unqualified being is simply the substance of a thing; the kind or sort of thing something is. Thus, the unqualified being of my son is human, while the unqualified being of my pet Miles is dog. But unqualified goodness works differently. Whereas the unqualified being of my son simply locates him in the appropriate kind without including any of his accidental features, to say appropriately that my son is good is to attribute more to him than mere inclusion in the right kind. To say that Julian is good is to say that he has those features that take a mere human to a good human. That is, to say that Julian is a good person (or a good human) is to say that Julian exemplifies his humanness to such-and-such a degree. The unqualified being of x thus differs from the unqualified goodness of x in the following way: x is an unqualified being just in case x exists, whereas x is unqualifiedly good just in case x exists and exemplifies the features distinctive of x's kind to such-and-such a degree.

Qualified being, on the other hand, includes accidental features of a thing. Julian is unqualifiedly human and qualifiedly Mexican. To say that Julian is Mexican is to add something to his unqualified being. Qualified goodness is similar to qualified being in that it, too, specifies that something is good in a certain respect. Thus, to say that Julian is unqualifiedly good is to say that he does not lack any feature that is supposed to be present in a human being, whereas to say that Julian is qualifiedly good is to say that he has some of the features that are supposed to be present in a human being, and to implicate that he does not have all of the features that are supposed to be present in a human being. If Julian's goodness is qualified in some way then he is not good unqualifiedly and hence does not possess all of the features that humans are supposed to have, or does not have them to the degrees that he should.

From these considerations it is easy to see that while "goodness" and "being" may refer to the same thing they do so under different descriptions or with different senses. Qualified and unqualified goodness pick out different sets of features, respectively, from qualified and unqualified being. Goodness picks out features that a thing is supposed to have in virtue of the kind of thing it is, whereas being picks out the features that a thing has, independently of any consideration as to whether the thing is supposed to have those features.

1.1 From GNF to CC

One way to motivate CC is by appeal to GNF. If the goodness of a thing depends on its nature, then in some way the nature of a thing circumscribes its goodness. That is, the nature of a thing places limitations on the kind(s) of goodness that the thing can (metaphysically) have. Another way of stating this connection is to say that the kind of being a thing is determines to some degree the kind of goodness a thing can have. Humans, in virtue of being the kind of being they are cannot have horse-goodness. Humans can only hope to achieve human goodness. So, at the very least, it looks as though we have some reason to think that goodness and being are linked in some way; the type of being x is determines the type of goodness x has or can have. We are still far from the claim that being is identical with goodness, but we are getting closer.

What we have at this stage is something like the following: the nature of a thing determines the properties it can and should have. The fact that my chair does not see is no defect in the chair because the chair's nature is not such that seeing is a feature that it either can or should have. The fact that I can barely see (without corrective lenses) is a defect in me because of the kind of thing I am. My nature is such that seeing (or being a seeing thing) is a property that I can and should have. Thus, I am good with respect to sight insofar as I possess the relevant property. But given GNF, there is no reason to restrict ourselves to such seemingly non-moral types of goodness. According to GNF, goodness is determined by the nature or function of the thing. Thus, Steve is a good human insofar as Steve exemplifies those features that belong to the nature of humans. To whatever degree Steve exemplifies those features, Steve is good to that same degree.

We can state the above using some of the terminology from Chapter 3. There we noted that "good" is a predicate-forming functor or a property-marker. To be a good K is to have the relevant properties of Ks. At this point, the connection between the attributive account of "good," its metaphysical corollary, and the convertibility thesis should be coming into sharper focus. Good Ks are just those members of K that possess or exemplify the features necessary for inclusion in K to such-and-such a degree. But this just is the convertibility thesis in a qualified form. x's goodness is a function of the features x has and the degree to which x exemplifies them. Goodness here is not a property of x, but is a way of describing or picking out the properties that x has. And this is good news for the defender of the convertibility thesis since it is unlikely that the thesis would make much sense were being itself a property.

At this stage, we have a limited form of the convertibility thesis. Being a good K is a matter of having the relevant features of K-hood to such-and-such a degree. Hence, good Ks are Ks with the features appropriate to K to such-and-such a degree. We can put this in a way that makes the connection to the convertibility thesis clearer and draws on some of the distinctions that were introduced earlier, when I discussed Aquinas's claim that being and goodness differ in sense. x is a good K just in case the being of x is qualified in such a way that x is not a mere member of K, but a member of K that exemplifies the features of K to such-and-such a degree. For example, Obama is a good president just in case Obama is the president and Obama possesses the features necessary for being a president to such-and-such a degree. To be the president Obama must possess certain features that everyone else currently lacks. To be a good president Obama must possess those features to such-and-such a degree. That is, and putting it in the terms of defenders of the convertibility thesis, Obama is the president just in case he has the potentialities relevant to being president, and he is a good president just in cases he has actualized those potentialities to such-and-such a degree.

Notice that the above account attempted to explain goodness not in terms of some *sui generis* property of goodness, but simply in terms of mundane, and seemingly non-normative, properties. That is, x is a good K just in case x possesses the being (the properties) that members of K are supposed to have. So, the goodness of a thing and the being of a thing are not distinct; to be good is to have a certain sort of being—the features that the kind specifies—to such-and-such a degree.

However, we do not yet have the full-fledged convertibility thesis. If the above account is correct, we can infer from GNF the claim that good Ks are simply Ks that have the relevant sort of being. Being a good K and having the relevant sort of properties are not distinct. Thus, being and goodness are identical at least insofar as we are considering what it takes to be a good K. But the convertibility thesis is stronger than what we have produced at this stage.

According to the convertibility thesis, being and goodness are identical. According to what I have argued thus far, a good K is identical with a K that has the relevant amount or type of being. But the convertibility thesis implies that if x is member of K, then x is good insofar as x exists, and regardless of whether x is a good K or not.

We can bridge the above gap by noting that in order for x to be a K x must have the requisite features (or be the relevant type of substance) for inclusion in K. Suppose that x is indeed a member of K. If x is a member of K, then x has features F, G, and H (where F, G, and H are sufficient for inclusion in K). Suppose that x is a member of some organic kind that normally matures through various stages. We can consider x at stage 1, 2, or n. At each stage, x will retain those features sufficient for inclusion in K, but as x progresses through various stages x will with gain additional features or increase the degree to which x exemplifies the features sufficient for inclusion in K. Consider x at stage 1, the initial stage of K-membership. At stage 1 x may be a good K qua stage 1, but a bad K qua stage 2. That is, at stage 1 x may be as x is supposed to be. Suppose at stage 1 that x is as x is supposed to be at stage 1. It is appropriate to call x a good K qua stage 1. But from what we have already seen, if x is a good K (qua stage 1), then x has the relevant sort of features that Ks are supposed to have to such-and-such a degree. Hence, if at stage 1 x is a good K then x has the relevant features of Ks to the relevant degree. Remember that according to the attributive account, the adjective "good" is a property-marker; it signals the presence of the relevant properties to the relevant degree. Now at stage 1, x is the barest sort of K possible. That is, at stage 1 x is an unqualified K. x is, at it were, a mere K. With one additional assumption we can bridge the gap between the above arguments and the full-fledged convertibility thesis.

The additional assumption needed is that for all x, if x exists, then there is some K that is x's primary kind, and if x were not K, then x would not exist.[2] Since at this stage, x is at the lowest level of K-hood, and it makes sense to say that x is a good K, it follows that being and goodness are identical.[3]

Here's the argument put a bit more formally.

1. x is a good K implies that x has the features relevant for being a member of K to such-and-such a degree.
2. Hence, being a good K is nothing over and above having the relevant features to such-and-such a degree.
3. Hence, being a good K is identical with being a K with features F, G, and H.
4. Hence, being and goodness are identical when considering a good K.
5. For all x, if x exists, then there is some primary kind K such that x is a member of K and x would cease to exist if x were not a member of K.
6. At stage 1 of x's existence, x has the features relevant for being a member of K.
7. Hence, at stage 1, x is a good K.
8. Stage 1 is the ontologically first stage.
9. Hence, x's existing is good.
10. Hence being and goodness are identical.

2 In Defense of the Privation Theory of Evil

In this section I will defend the following:

Privation Claim (PC): If "good" and "bad" are attributive, then the privation theory of evil is true.

PC is related to CC in that the privation theory of evil is true if, and only if, the convertibility thesis is true. Thus, if I can establish PC then I will have demonstrated, albeit indirectly, that CC is true as well.

In Section 1.1 I argued that CC is true, and I did little to defend the idea that goodness and being are identical. In this section I argue that the attributive account of "good" and "bad" implies the privation theory of evil, and since the privation theory is quite controversial (to say the least) I will need to defend it. After all, if the arguments of this section are sound and the attributive account does indeed imply the privation theory of evil, and if the privation theory of evil is false, then the attributive account is false as well. Since many contemporary philosophers think that the privation theory of evil is false, I will need to spend some time defending it against common objections. Thus, this section will take up a defense of PC and its consequent.

2.1 Explaining the Privation Theory of Evil and Avoiding Some Confusions

For all of its historical pedigree, the privation theory of evil (hereafter, PTE) is not popular today. However, PTE is often misunderstood and such misunderstanding is often based on an attempt to understand and criticize it without seeing PTE in its proper framework. I believe that PTE is best understood within a framework that explicitly affirms the convertibility of being and goodness—is virtue theoretic in terms of normativity—and maintains something like the analogy of being.

According to the privation theory of evil, evil (or badness in general) is the absence of a good that is supposed to be present (I take this to be equivalent to another way of putting the doctrine—evil is the privation of a due good). Hence, evil is both metaphysically and epistemically parasitic on goodness. That is, given the privation theory, goodness is ontologically and epistemically more fundamental or basic than evil. Goodness is more fundamental ontologically because if there is evil there must be goodness, but the converse is false. Goodness is more epistemically fundamental, because grasping the notion of evil requires grasping the notion of goodness, whereas the converse is false.

Perhaps the most common confusion associated with PTE is that it denies the existence of evil. But, as others have noted, PTE does no such thing. PTE is an attempt to explain the nature of evil. According to PTE, evil is the lack or privation of a due good. If there really is such lack in some object or some action, then there really is something bad (or evil; I will use bad and evil interchangeably unless explicitly noted). But we must be careful not to reify the badness. Thomas Aquinas, who has the most influential and undoubtedly the most developed account of PTE, recognizes the confusion and its potential. He writes:

> As is said in the 5th book of the Metaphysics "being" is used in two ways. In one sense it means the being of a thing; in this sense it is divided by the ten categories,

and we can use the word if and only if we can use the word "thing." In this sense no deprivation is a being, and hence evil is not a being. In another sense we use "being" to signify the truth of a proposition which consists in a composition that we indicate by using the "is"; this is the sense of "being" which corresponds to the questions "Is it the case that . . .?" It is in this sense that we say that blindness is in the eye, or that any other deprivation is wherever it is. And it is in this sense that evil is said to be. On account of their ignorance of this distinction, some people, realizing that some things are rightly said to be bad, and that evil said to be in things, have supposed that evil is a sort of thing itself.[4]

What Aquinas appears to be getting at is the distinction between the truth of some statement or proposition and the conditions of the statement's truth. What makes the statement "Dogs bark" true is a different thing from what makes the statement "Dogs are four-legged" true. The things that make the statements true are, in these cases, real features of the world. But what makes the statement "Adolph is a wicked man" true is not some positive reality. Rather Adolph's wickedness consists in Adolph's turning toward lesser goods than the good that Adolph ought to be pursuing. In the section responding to objections to the PTE we will spend some more time on moral evil, but the important point to secure here is that the statement "Adolph is a wicked man" may very well be true. That is, PTE does not claim it is never true to say that such-and-such is bad. Rather PTE claims that the truth-conditions of such statements will involve absences of some sort, where the sort of absence depends on the kind of things in question.

So, it is true to say of some things or actions that they are bad, according to PTE. The badness attributed, however, will always be kind-relative. Some object O is bad in such-and-such a way just in case O lacks some feature that O is supposed to have. The idea that O is supposed to have some feature is itself a kind-relative notion. O is supposed to have feature F just in case O belongs to some kind K such that Ks in general have F or flourishing (or well-functioning) members of K are F. For example, while it is true that my desk fails to see, this failing is not sufficient for attributing blindness to my desk. Blindness is a defect in anything that has it, and it is no defect of my desk that it fails to see. Why? Well, desks are not the sorts of thing that are supposed to see. It is not in the nature of a desk to see things. What makes a desk a desk has nothing to do with seeing. That is why it is appropriate to say of some human who cannot see that she/he is blind. Sight is a feature humans are supposed to have. (i.e. humankind in general has the feature of seeing or at least flourishing members of humankind do).[5]

Interestingly the above attempt to avoid confusion nicely reinforces one of the claims made in Chapter 2. "Bad," like "good," is attributive. Just as it does not make sense to say that x is good apart from some explicit or implicit understanding of the sort of thing x is, it does not make sense to say of something *y* that it is bad apart from the same explicit or implicit understanding. Nothing is bad full stop.

2.2 *From Attributive to Privation*

In Chapter 2 it was argued that "bad," like "good," is attributive. According to Geach, "bad" is something like an *alienans* adjective. *Alienans* adjectives have two features. First, it is invalid to split an *alienans* adjective from the noun it modifies. Second, what is true of the noun minus the *alienans* is not necessarily true of the noun plus *alienans*. The first feature is enough to ensure that "bad" is an attributive adjective, but the second feature shows that the attributive nature of "bad" implies badness is a privation.

According to PTE, evil is the absence of some feature that *should* be present. Notice that the privation account does not claim that evil is the mere absence of something. I am not bad because I lack x-ray vision. X-ray vision is not a feature that is supposed to be present in a being like me. The privation account assumes that we can come to know what features a things can and should have.

Evil is the absence of a *feature* that should be present in some substance. The privation theory of evil denies that it is possible for something to be wholly bad. If evil is the privation of something that ought to be present, then the thing that ought to be present must be some property of a substance.[6] There are, as far as I can tell, two main reasons for claiming that evil is the absence of a feature and not some other sort of absence. First, the privation account is equivalent to the convertibility thesis, and implies that being is good. But it is hard to make sense of the idea that there are substances that ought to be present. What, we might ask, should these substances be present in? Where should they be present? Suppose it is bad for the Dallas Cowboys to lack their quarterback. A quarterback should be present on the field, and thus the lack of a quarterback makes the Cowboys a bad football team (at least in this respect). But a quarterback is not, properly speaking, a substance. A quarterback is a qualified substance. The notion of substance at work in the privation theory of evil corresponds nicely with the notion of substance used in previous section's argument for the convertibility thesis. The notion of substance countenanced by the privation account is one of a *primary* substance, and nothing is primarily a quarterback. While it is perfectly intelligible to say it is bad for the Cowboys to lack a quarterback, this badness is really just the Cowboys lacking a feature they should have. The team lacks the feature of having a quarterback on the field. While this is only one example, I think it is fairly clear how to generalize to other cases. The mere absence of a substance is not an evil. Rather, evil is always the absence of some feature in a substance (or, given the Cowboys example, the absence of some feature in a collection of substances).

Perhaps you are not convinced by the above argument. We can use the convertibility thesis in another way to get to the same place. Assume the convertibility thesis is true. If being and goodness are identical, then badness cannot be a being of any sort. So, badness must be some sort of non-being. But it is implausible to think that badness is simply non-being. If any non-being at all counted as a badness, there would be much more badness in the word than is plausible to suppose, because every non-existence would be bad. The absence of dishes in my pocket, bullets in my mouth, spikes in my eyes, trees in my bed, unicorns, etc., would be bad. So, badness is not simply non-being. Rather, badness is the lack of a being that is supposed to be present. But if badness is not simply non-being, then it does not make sense to say that there are *substances* that ought to be present. If there were substances that ought to be present, then their absence would be bad, and we would be right back at the position that badness is simply non-being. Badness is the absence of a non-substance that should be present. That is, badness is the absence of some feature of a substance that is supposed to be present.

Notice that x can lack a feature that xs are supposed to have, in virtue of having features that xs are not supposed to have. My watch is a bad watch because it does not tell time accurately. But my watch does not tell time accurately, because it was submerged in water and it is not water resistant. The water in my watch is not an absence. But in virtue of the presence of water in my watch, my watch lacks what should be present (namely, the ability to tell time accurately). McCabe writes to the same effect:

> [B]adness is a negative thing. Please notice that this does *not* mean that a bad washing machine always has to have a part missing—it is not negative in that sense. A washing machine may be bad not only because it has too little, as when there is no driving belt on the spin drier, but also because it has too much, as when someone has filled the interior with glue. Badness is negative just in the sense that a bad thing doesn't succeed in measuring up to our expectations. Badness, then, is always a defect, an absence, in this sense.[7]

Another consequence of the privation theory of evil and the attributive account of "bad" is the particularity of evils.[8] The badness of x will not generally resemble the badness of y, especially if x and y are members of different kinds. A bad heart is one that fails to pump blood (or fails to do so efficiently, etc.), whereas a bad eye is one that fails to see properly. The first lack is altogether different from the second. The particularity of badness even extends to members of the same kind. This bad heart may be quite different from that one; this bad friend may be quite different from that one; and so on and on. Given the attributive account of "bad," none of this is surprising. Badness is always relative to a kind, and for many kinds there will be quite a number of different ways to fail to be a flourishing member of the kind. Thus, there is no nature or essence of badness.

We are now in a position to see that the attributive account of "bad" implies the privation theory of evil. According to the attributive account of "bad," the statement "x is bad" is either elliptical for "x is a bad K" or is semantically incomplete. Thus, badness is always attached to some substantive, something with a nature or function. To say that x is a bad K is to say that x is not a thriving member of the kind to which it belongs. x's badness consists in x's not exemplifying the features that members of K should exemplify (or x's not exemplifying those features determinative of Ks to such-and-such a degree). On the attributive account of badness, it does not make sense to say that x is wholly bad. The only way that x could be wholly bad is if x were just bad simpliciter and not a bad K. But the only way that x could be bad simpliciter is if "bad" is not attributive. Hence, if it is possible for something to be bad simpliciter (simply bad and not a bad K), then the attributive account of "bad" (and its metaphysical corollary) is false, and by contraposition, if the attributive account of "bad" is true, then it is not possible for something to be bad simpliciter. If something is bad, then it is bad in a certain respect. The badness of x is parasitic on its goodness. Notice that this is one of the main claims of PTE.

Bad members of K are members that do not possess the relevant features to the relevant degree. I take it that this account of badness is what Geach had in mind when he claimed that "bad" is something like an *alienans* adjective.[9] A bad K is still a K, but it is a K that is failing in some way. A bad K is a K such that the true statements made of normal Ks or good Ks are not all true with respect to it, and this is just the similarity to *alienans* adjectives that Geach mentioned.

Moving from the attributive account of "bad" to PTE was fairly straightforward. We can also move from PTE to the convertibility thesis. If PTE is true, then so is the convertibility thesis. If x is not a bad K, then there are no features x should have but does not. But, if there are no features x should have but does not, then x has all of the features it is supposed to have, and thus x is a good K. That is, since evil is the absence of some feature that should be present, the absence of evil is equivalent to the absence of an absence of some feature that should be present, which is equivalent to the presence of some feature that should be present, which is being and hence goodness.

But now we encounter an obstacle. For many PTE is clearly false, in which case the attributive account must be false as well. So, if the attributive account is to stand, we must confront some of the main reasons for rejecting PTE. In the sections that follow, I will present and respond to two different objections to PTE.

2.3 The Pain Objection

The privationist seems to have a fairly easy time explaining some bad events, actions, and substances in terms of various kinds of absences. As we have seen, blindness is plausibly captured by privation analyses, and similar stories can be told about lying, stealing, and adultery, for example. But other paradigmatic bad things seem to elude a privation account. For example, it appears obvious that pain is bad, but it is far from obvious that the badness of pain can be located in the absence of some feature that should be present.

As Todd Calder points out:

> The problem is that in some cases evil is not just the absence of goodness but rather some positively bad existing property or quality, and thus, the privation account of evil cannot characterize all forms of evil.... [P]ain is not simply the absence of feeling or pleasure, it is a positively bad sensation or feeling. The absence of feeling or pleasure is numbness or experiential paralysis; it is akin to the way a body feels under local anaesthetic. Pain, on the other hand, is a felt quality, one that we typically try to avoid.[10]

I think it is fair to say that the pain objection is the most common one raised against the privation account of badness. I hope to show that this objection should be put to rest.

Calder and others[11] seem to assume that the painfulness of a pain sensation is something that all pain sensations have in common. Perhaps the most common view here (at least in recent times) is that painfulness is some sort of quale, and, as such, it is essentially bad. As we shall see below, there are strong reasons for denying that painfulness is a quale, but before considering those, I want to consider a response to the pain objection that lets the quale assumption stand.[12]

Suppose then that the painfulness of a sensory pain is an object of some sort. Murat Aydede expresses this as follows: "When I feel pain in my hand, it seems that I have a sensory experience that prompts me to attribute something to the back of my hand by deploying my concept PAIN.... Indeed, it seems as if I apply PAIN to something in my hand."[13] A pain seems to be a quality that is essentially owned, in the sense that "[t]here cannot be a pain with no one or no creature around to feel the pain."[14] So pains are thought to be qualities that do not have an independent existence. But we have the resources to accommodate this assumption and still respond to this version of the pain objection.

If pain is a quality of some sort, then it is a being of some sort, and as such, given the convertibility thesis it is good. Now, it does seem possible for there to be defective pains. Consider phantom limb pain and referred pain cases. As Michael Tye notes, "Pains, viewed as experiences, intuitively can be misleading or inaccurate."[15] Tye mentions the case of phantom limb pain as an example of hallucination, and referred pain as an example of illusion. These seem to be pains that misrepresent, and, hence, fail in various ways. These types of cases show that we can distinguish between good pains and bad pains qua qualities. A pain is a bad pain qua pain-kind just in case it is a defective member of the pain-kind. Phantom limb pain and referred pains are great examples of bad pains in the sense under discussion. Good pains, then, are those that are not defective qua members of the pain-kind. That is, good pains do what pains are supposed to, which, for a representationalist such as Tye, means they represent tissue damage or the potential for such damage.

Remember that we are presently considering the view that the painfulness of pain is an object of some sort. But even if this painfulness is not an object but instead an experience that a subject undergoes, one can still think of the experience as being veridical or not and as successful or defective in some way. The badness that the human undergoes is the result of the pain doing precisely what it is supposed to do. If this is plausible, then there is no problem for the privation account. The privationist can plausibly locate the badness in some absence, such as the lack of normal functioning or normal consciousness or well-being, and affirm that pains do have positive aspects to them.

"Too fast," says the objector. The badness of the pain is the feeling of it, and the feeling of the pain is a positive feature of the agent undergoing it. The above attempt to overcome the pain objection really misses the point of the pain objection. That there are privations that can be identified in cases of pain is not to the point. Pains indicate a lack of function or well-being in the organism that has them. But pains are more than that. The badness of a pain is something over and above the badness that a pain may indicate (say, the badness that brings about the pain). "The pain is caused by the absence, it does not consist in it."[16] To repeat, the badness of a pain is the feeling of it; its badness lies in its phenomenology, and its phenomenology is essential to it or at least intrinsic to it. Thus pains are essentially or, at least, intrinsically bad.

The attributive account of "bad" claims there is no such thing as simple badness. The pain objection is sometimes put as if there were such a thing as simple badness. But, we must ask, what precisely is bad here? The pain may be a fully functioning member of the pain kind, playing its biological role exactly as it should. So the pain is not bad qua member of the pain-kind. That is, the pain, considered as a member of its kind, is quite good. (Obviously, we are ignoring defective pains). Here again, the attributive account can shed light on the issue.

One of the tests used in Chapter 2 to demonstrate the attributive nature of "good" and "bad" was the Higher-Order and Lower-Order Kinds Test. From the fact that x is a good K and all Ks are K^* (where K^* may be a higher-order or lower-order kind) it does not follow that x is a good K^*. So, from the facts that x is a good pain and pains are sensations, it does not follow that x is a good sensation. x may be a pain that performs the function or role of pain quite well, and perhaps for that very reason, x is a bad feeling or sensation. "[P]ain is not simply the absence of feeling or pleasure, it is a positively bad sensation or feeling."[17] But we need to be careful here. Given the lessons learned from the attributive account, the ambiguity of the statement "pain is a bad sensation or feeling" should be obvious. The statement might mean (a) that pain is a sensation that lacks certain features sensations should have in virtue of their membership in the sensation-kind, or (b) that pain is a sensation or feeling that is bad for a human or animal to sense or feel. That (a) and (b) are quite different is clear from the fact that some sensation s may be bad according to (a) but not bad according to (b), and bad according to (b) but not bad according to (a). For example, I might believe I see my wife in the distance, but because I am not wearing my glasses I am mistaken. Thus, my sense of sight, and the visual sensation I have, are bad according to (a). But the apparent sensing of my wife in the distance is not bad to feel or to sense. Thus, it is not bad according to (b). I think it is clear that Calder and others have the (b) reading in mind when they say that pain is a bad sensation or feeling.

If the claim is that all instances of pain are bad for some creature to feel, then the claim appears to be false. There are examples where pain is desirable, such as the satisfying pain of a strenuous workout. But there are also less controversial cases where pain is felt but not felt as unpleasant or bad. "The view that pain has distinct sensory and affective–emotional components, subserved by different neural mechanisms, was first proposed by Melzack and Casey in 1968, and in the thirty years or so years since then it has been shown to be well motivated by both a wealth of clinical data and neuroscientific evidence."[18] So, pain is not *essentially* bad to feel or sense. The affective component of pain can be divorced from the sensory component.

Nevertheless, there are plenty of cases where the experience of pain is bad to feel. But given that the affective and sensory components of pain can be divorced, it is natural to think that the badness that is felt has something to do with our attitude toward the sensation.

One way the privationist can handle the fact that it is often bad to feel or sense pain without denying that pain is a positive reality and not itself an absence is by remembering that PTE is not committed to the claim that a bad K is bad solely in virtue of missing something that should be present. PTE is compatible with the idea that x is a bad K, not because x is missing some part, but because some positive feature is present. John's hand is defective not because he is missing fingers, but because he has too many of them. Sally's car is defective not because it is missing spark plugs, but because the engine is filled with them. Now, these additional parts will be responsible for some feature that is lacking but should be present. However, the important point here is that it is in virtue of too many parts that the hand and the car are bad and not in virtue of having too few/missing parts.

So, the positive features of pain—the feeling of it, its phenomenology—may themselves be responsible for the lack that actually accounts for the badness of feeling pain. This account is especially plausible if we are strong representationalists, though, as we shall see, one need not be a strong representationalist to endorse this response.

The strong representationalist identifies the phenomenal character of pain with the phenomenal content of pain, and ties phenomenal content with representational content. As Tye describes, "The phenomenal character of a given pain, on my view, is one and the same as the phenomenal content it has. The phenomenal content of a pain is a species of representational content."[19] Thus, the phenomenal character of a pain experience is a representation of something.

Few deny that pains have a representational aspect. As we saw earlier, pains can succeed or fail to represent and, as such, can properly be described as bad or good qua members of the pain-kind. The strong representationalist argues that the best account of the phenomenology of pain is to identify it with the representational content of pain. Tye's representationalism offers the PTE advocate a ready response to the pain objection:

> Pain is normally very unpleasant. People in pain try to get rid of it or to diminish it. Why? The answer surely is because pain *feels* unpleasant or bad, because it is *experienced* as such. But what exactly is experienced as unpleasant? One's attention, when one feels pain, goes to a place different from the one in which the experience of pain is located. The disturbance that is experienced as unpleasant is located in the bodily location to which one attends (in normal circumstances). People whose pains lack the affective dimension undergo purely sensory, non-evaluative representations of tissue damage of one sort or another in a localized bodily region. Those whose pains are normal experience the same sort of disturbance, but now it is experienced by them as unpleasant or bad. It is precisely *because* this is the case that normal subjects have the cognitive reactions to pain they do, reactions such as desiring to stop the pain.
>
> To experience tissue damage as bad is to undergo an experience that represents that damage as bad. Accordingly, in my view, the affective dimension of pain is as much a part of the representational content of pain as the sensory dimension is.[20]

The strong representationalist views the negative or unpleasant phenomenal content of a pain experience as being just as representational as the merely sensory phenomenal content. The evaluative phenomenal content represents the bodily damage as bad, whereas the non-evaluative phenomenal content simply represents the bodily damage, without representing it as bad. Given what we said earlier, it would seem that when the sensory and affective components of pain are together (what Tye calls the normal circumstances), the representational content of the pain experience more accurately represents what is actually happening (or has happened or is about to happen) than when these components are not together.

The affective phenomenal content is not, according to the strong representationalist, something over and above the representational content of the pain experience. The privationist can thus adopt a version of strong representationalism and easily accommodate sensory pain.

The very real unpleasant phenomenal content of most pain experiences represents one's bodily integrity as being undermined in some way. The phenomenal content is the representation of a privation of some sort. The unpleasant feeling of pain is just the evaluative content of most pain experiences and partly constitutes the representational content of the experience. Since the representational content of the experience is a representation of some sort of bodily damage, the unpleasant feeling is itself a representation of some sort of bodily damage under the guise of an evaluation of that damage. There is nothing here that threatens PTE and, if strong representationalism or something like it is the correct account of pain experiences, then the pain objection fails.

But perhaps strong representationalism is false. Rather than present and respond to the various criticisms that have been made against strong representationalism, I want to consider another way of conceiving pains and the unpleasant feeling associated with them. Doing so will show that PTE is not committed to strong representationalism even though it seems to be a clear ally. My goal is not to defend these accounts of the nature of pain. Rather, my goal is to show that there are a few competing accounts of the nature of pain that are each compatible with PTE. PTE does not entail a particular conception of pain.

Assume that the unpleasant feeling of normal pain experiences is not representational, contra strong representationalism. This assumption, it would seem, places the ball back into the pain objector's court. Since the unpleasant aspect of the feeling of pain no longer represents the tissue damage in the way the sensory aspect may, the PTE advocate must locate the badness of the unpleasant feeling elsewhere without thereby reifying the badness. We will consider two different ways the privationist may cope with denials of strong representationalism.

Colin Klein has argued that representationalism about pains is false. Klein presents an imperative theory of pain, according to which, rather than having representational content pains have imperative content.

Klein argues that sensations such as hunger, thirst, itches, and pains are imperative sensations:

> Hunger demands that I eat; thirst demands that I drink. Note the features common to all of these sensations. Each carries little information about either its cause or about what future state of the world would be required to alleviate it. Indeed, all display a curious failure even to localize precisely, and (like thirst) can be felt as imperatives that issue from nowhere in particular at all. The distinctive qualities of each stems from the fact that they demand a certain kind of action to be satisfied.[21]

Imperative sensations do not represent the world as being a certain way, but instead make demands on their owners. Since pain is, according to Klein, an imperative sensation, it too makes demands on its owner. "The content of any pain is a negative imperative.... What unifies... pains is the imperative that I stop doing what I am doing; their content is a proscription against action."[22]

A particular pain commands against taking or continuing certain actions. The actions should not be taken or continued. Such is the content of pain. As such, the unpleasantness of pain is explained. Indeed, it is the unpleasantness of the pain that is the imperative content.

> The imperative content of pains exhausts what there is to say about pain. This is meant in support of the intentionalist. The phenomenal properties of pain are exhausted by their imperative content, and nothing more need be cited to account for the qualitative feel of pains. The different between someone in pain and some not in pain is just the presence or absence of an imperative. Give me enough morphine for my pain to be lessened, and you lessen the strength of that imperative. Give me enough to eliminate my pain, and you have eliminated the imperative against action entirely.[23]

The unpleasantness of the pain experience has imperative force. The pain experience commands against various actions in virtue of the unpleasantness of the pain experience. The phenomenal content of the pain is just the proscription against taking a certain range of actions. So, the privationist needs to argue either that (a) the proscription itself is a privation, and hence so are the phenomenal properties, or (b) the proscription is not a privation, but this is not damaging to the privationist.

I think option (b) is the most promising here. Pain sensations are identical to negative commands, and negative commands are proscriptions against doing such-and-such. Hence, pain sensations, including their phenomenology, are proscriptions against doing such-and-such. The experience itself is a command against. While the command is not an absence but a positive entity, the content of the command is. Thus, the content of the pain is an absence as well.

Perhaps an analogy will help here. I tell my daughter to clean her room. I have issued a command. The content of my command is something positive; it is a demand that a certain set of actions be performed. Suppose I tell my daughter to stop yelling. I have issued a command, but this time the command is negative; it is a demand that a certain action not be performed. I am demanding the cessation of something just as pains, according to the imperative theory, are demanding the cessation of something.

Unpleasant pains demand the cessation of something. They demand the absence of some feature. The pain, in effect, says, "get rid of this feature right now." The unpleasantness of pain is thus a positive reality demanding the absence of a certain range of actions. "On an imperative view, the primary role of pain is to limit action by commanding against using your body in certain ways. This is a good way to achieve the biological end of feeling pain. [The] important function [of pain] requires that they command against movement contrary to health."[24] The phenomenal content of pain is captured by the cessation of action being demanding by the pain. Pain feels bad precisely because the command is not being obeyed. But if that is all there is to pain's phenomenal content, and hence to the badness of the sensation, then the badness is a type of absence. The pain is, in effect, telling me to stop, and if I do not heed it the pain continues. My failure to obey explains the badness of the sensation, and, of course, a failure to obey is a privation. Hence, the imperative theory of pain is compatible with PTE.

Another theory of pain that is not representational but is compatible with the privation theory denies that the painfulness of pain is a quale. We have already seen some reasons why we should separate the sensory and affective components of pain, but there are still other reasons.

Pain asymbolia syndrome represents what seems to be a counterexample to the idea that the sensation of pain itself is bad. That is, in pain asymbolia syndrome, the sensation of pain and the negative feeling come apart.

> There is . . . quite substantial scientific evidence that there are abnormal pain phenomena where the sensory and affective aspects of pain experiences are disassociated from each other. . . . The most typical case is known as the pain asymbolia syndrome, where people who suffer from it have pain experiences without the negative affect. Interestingly, these people still identify their experience as pain, but show no bodily, emotional, and behavioral signs typically associated with the unpleasant aspect of pains. They are feeling a pain that doesn't hurt![25]

Such cases seem to show that the unpleasantness or badness of pain is neither essential nor intrinsic to it. Rather the badness of pain is extrinsic and plausibly lies in our aversion to the sensation.

Austen Clark uses the fact that the sensory and affective components of pain can be separated to argue that the badness of pain is not a quale.

> Now pains are very often taken to be [a] paradigm example . . . of states that manifest qualia. I have no wish to deny that episodes of pain typically have some sort of sensory character. But I do want to deny that what makes these episodes *painful* is a quale. Painfulness is not, and could not be, a quale. Pains have a sensory character, but it is not their sensory character—specifically, not their qualitative character—that makes them so awful. So as paradigm examples of qualia they leave something to be desired.[26]

Clark's argument against the claim that the painfulness or awfulness of pain is a quale is that the only common characteristic of pain experiences that are unpleasant is their unpleasantness. Other than the aversion one has to the experience, nothing else need be had in common. But this feature of painfulness suggests that the painfulness is not to be found in some sensory quality, but rather in one's attitude toward a sensory quality. "A cramp or a pinprick might be equally painful, even if no sensory quality is common to the two episodes. . . . Perhaps the essential property in virtue of which two episodes are both painful is not any sensory quality at all, but simply the undesirability of whatever collection of such qualities they happen to manifest."[27] So, once we allow for the separation of the sensory character of a pain sensation from the affective character of that same sensation, the most plausible view is that the painfulness of pain is not a quale at all. If that is right, then it is misleading to say that a pain sensation is a bad sensation. The badness is not located in the sensation, since the sensation is not the locus of the unpleasantness or awfulness. Rather, the badness is located in the fact that the sensation one is currently undergoing is undesirable.

Consider in this regard Mark Murphy's recent attempt to defuse the pain objection:

> The only really persuasive instance of a positive evil that I know of is that of pain, which seems not at all like a deprivation but like a genuine, on-its-own-account evil. But I say that even pain, when its basic badness is made manifest, is privation of good. For what is bad about pain is its being unwanted; as Parfit writes, we would regard drugs that made us no longer mind the sensation of pain as effective analgesics (1984, p. 501). It is wrong to say that a sensation of pain is an evil, bad for one, if one has that sensation yet does not dislike it. The evil of pain, as I see it, is its being a privation of a genuine good: that of inner peace, the state of having only fulfilled desires. Pain, a sensation characteristically accompanied by a desire not to have it, is a disruption from a lack in the good of inner peace. And so pain does not constitute an ultimately plausible counterexample to the notion that all evil is privation of good.[28]

It is not the mere sensation that is bad, but rather the fact that I do not want to be having such a sensation that is the badness of pain. In this way the positive features of the pain can be accommodated without sacrificing PTE.

In this section we have considered three different conceptions of the nature of pain and found that on all three the badness of pain can be accounted for in a manner consistent with PTE. Thus, the pain objection should, at best, be considered much more controversial than it seems to be, or, at worst, tossed aside.

2.4 The Wicked Objection

The final objection to consider against the privation theory claims that certain instances of moral evil cannot be explained by the privationist. This objection can be dealt with much more quickly than the previous one. Once again, I find Todd Calder's way of stating the objection perspicuous.

Calder considers the defense of PTE by Anglin and Goetz against the objection from wickedness and finds it wanting.[29] According to Anglin and Goetz, moral evils are to be understood as "the nonfulfillment of duties. For instance, the evils of murder and of letting starving people in distant countries die consist in the nonfulfillment of the duties to respect and preserve life."[30] So far so good, but now we need a way to distinguish between the two cases, because many would regard murder as more evil than letting starving people in distant countries die. It is at this juncture that Calder tries to locate a problem for the privationist. He says:

> ... the only way to account for why murder is a greater nonfulfillment of the duty to respect and preserve life is to refer to the intrinsic disvalue of attributes possessed by the murderer such as her intention and desire to take someone else's life without justification. But these are attributes she possess, not privations, and thus it seems that even if we describe murder as the nonfulfillment of the duty to respect and preserve life, to distinguish it from other, less evil, forms of failing this duty, we cannot characterize it solely in terms of the privation of good properties or attributes.[31] (Calder, 374)

Calder anticipates an objection. The privationist will likely reply to the above that Calder himself has identified where the privation, and hence the badness, of the murder lies along with its difference from letting starving people die in distant countries. As Calder states, the badness of murder can be located in the desire and intention to take someone else's life without justification. Thus, the positive features—the desire and intention to take someone else's life—are not where the badness is found. Rather, the badness is found in the fact that the action is lacking a feature—justification—that it should have. Calder responds thusly:

> For instance, to adequately characterize murder we must say more than that murder is the nonfulfillment of the duty to refrain from unjustified killing: we must say what it is to fail to refrain from unjustified killing. To do so, we must say what it is to kill without justification. But we cannot say what it is to kill without justification without reference to attributes possessed by the murderer, such as her beliefs, desires and intentions. But if our analysis makes reference to attributes possessed by the murderer, we no longer have a privation theory of evil.[32]

I am perplexed by this response. Calder does not seem to realize that the privationist *is committed* to making "reference to attributes possessed by the murderer" when explaining of the badness of murder. Indeed, the privationist is committed to making reference to attributes possessed by whatever it is whose badness is being explained. The privationist maintains that badness is parasitic on goodness in the sense that the only way for something to be bad is for it to lack something it should have. But being parasitic on good in this way implies that there is something good present.

So, the privationist, in order to give a full account of the badness of some action or person, must appeal to various traits of the action or person and explain how the badness is parasitic on these. For example, if an action is bad it is an action of some sort that is bad, and the badness will be parasitic on the goodness of the action considered by itself. The act of stealing a car involves, among things, various desires to obtain transportation, or money or whatever, and these are, considered apart from the badness of stealing, good things to desire. Thus, there is no badness in a thing without goodness, though the converse is false. This is simply what PTE says about badness.

So the privationist should not be embarrassed by needing to make reference to attributes possessed by the murderer (or any other bad thing), because that is what PTE entails. The murderer desires and intends various things that are not bad in themselves, but are bad when the desires and intentions lack a feature or features (such as justification) that should be present.

3 Arguments for God's Existence

3.1 From Semantic and Metaphysical Unity

One might worry that if the semantic and metaphysical accounts of Chapters 2 and 4 are correct, then attributions of goodness to members of different kinds share nothing significant in common. For example, a good horse and a good pen do not seem to possess very many properties in common. This suggests that attributions of goodness to things that are not members of the same kind would be ambiguous and would imply a sort of semantic relativism. But surely it is false that "good" is as ambiguous as the attributive account seems to imply. Hence, the attributive account is false.

There are at least two ways to respond to this objection. First, as we have seen, the semantic and metaphysical accounts of goodness imply that goodness and being are convertible. If the attributive account implies the convertibility theory, then the kind of semantic relativism with which the present objection is concerned does not arise. All attributions of goodness turn out to refer to the same thing—namely, being. Of course, the kind of being that is relevant will differ from case to case. For example, the kind of being that is needed to take my laptop from a mediocre one to a good one is quite different from the kind of being that is needed to take my car from a broken down one to a running one. Given that the kind of thing something is circumscribes the kind of goodness it can acquire, it is not surprising that the kind of thing something is circumscribes the kind of being it can and should acquire. It is a virtue of the attributive account that it predicts that goodness and being are relative in this way, and not, as the present objection would have it, a vice.

Nevertheless, the objection can be re-phrased in terms of semantic relativism with respect to the term "being." I think the objection has less force at this level, but less force is still force. The next response will help reduce the force to nil.

The second way to respond to the present objection is by introducing God into one's metaethics. Attributions of goodness would still pick out different features in different kinds of things. Nevertheless, with God as creator and the end of all creation, each thing's function or nature will be directed in its own way toward God, the Good itself. God would then serve as the unifier of all of the diverse attributions of goodness.

Assume that x is good iff x is a good K. But for different Ks, x will be good in different ways. As just noted, this consequence may lead some to think that attributions of goodness to members of different Ks will imply a kind of semantic relativism where "good" never means the same thing. If the attributive account is correct, and if semantic relativism is false, then there must be something that unifies all of our various attributions of goodness in such a way that "good" is neither univocal nor equivocal. Thus, attributions of goodness would seem to fall into the category of analogical predication, where the only candidate unifier is something that all Ks (or things with functions or natures) are directed toward: something in which they have their end ultimately satisfied. This ultimate satisfier of ends, to which all things are directed, is what we call God.

The above argument is much too quick to satisfy most. But I think the basic ingredients are enough to help us develop some more sophisticated versions of it.

3.2 From Analogy

The attributive account of "good" implies one of the following: attributions of goodness are univocal, equivocal, or they are analogous. Clearly attributions of goodness are not univocal on this account. Recall that "good" is best understood as a property-marker or predicate forming functor. If x is a good K and y is a good K^*, then those features that make x a good K differ from those that make y a good K^*. Thus, attributions of goodness to x and to y will pick out different features. Hence "goodness" is not univocal. Assuming that semantic relativism is false for "good," attributions of goodness cannot be equivocal. Thus, attributions of goodness must be analogical. They are related in some way but differ in the respects pointed out above.[33]

If "good" is an analogical term, then there is some one thing to which all attributions of goodness are related. That is, analogy assumes that there is a focal meaning, a non-analogous application of the analogous term to which all other applications are related.[34] The famous health example illustrates this point. One's dinner is healthy in a way that one's complexion is not, and yet, it is often appropriate to call both healthy. Eschewing equivocation leads us to posit something that unifies these diverse but related uses of the term "health." The most plausible unifier here is the relevant organism (or kind of organism). The dinner is healthy in that it contributes to the health of the organism, while the complexion is healthy not by contributing to the health of the organism but by being evidence of the health of the organism. Both uses of "health" are, thus, analogous uses since both pick out features that are related, albeit in different ways, to one single thing: the proper functioning or well-being of the organism.

Attributions of health to various items are unified by being tied to one item to which they all, in some way, point. If "good" is an analogous term, then it is reasonable to expect that attributions of goodness to various items are unified by being tied to one thing to which all the attributions in some way point.

In the case of the term "health," each of the non-focal uses of the term were such that the application of being healthy was not to the item in question but to something else, namely, the organism. The dinner is not itself healthy, but is a means to health. The complexion is not itself healthy, but is a sign of health in the organism.

In the case of the term "good," the non-focal uses of the term are *not* such that the application of goodness is not to the item in question but to something else. That is, unlike the term "healthy," the term "good" is typically applied to the thing itself. This difference between the analogical terms "health" and "good" forces us to find the focal meaning of the term "good" in something quite different from where we would find it for "health."

Focal uses of the term "health" refer to an organism, whereas non-focal uses do not refer to organisms, and this difference is explained by the fact that the things referred to in non-focal uses of "health" are not really healthy at all. The only thing that really can be healthy is the organism. For "good" the case is different. "Good" is an analogical term, but when it is used in a non-focal way the things that are said to be good may nevertheless be good, considered by themselves. Thus, it would be a mistake to attempt to locate the focal meaning of "good" in an organism, the way that we do with "health."

It is instructive to think of Aristotle's ten categories here, if only for illustrative purposes. It is appropriate to apply the term "good" to items that are members of distinct categories. Substances can be good, as can qualities, relations, quantities, etc. Furthermore, items falling in these different categories can, it seems, be good independently of their relation to items in the other categories. There are good qualities, good relations, good places, etc. Thus, the focal meaning of "good" cannot be a member of one of the categories. If it were, then we would have a situation similar to what we find with the term "health," where the focal meaning is a member of just one category. The focal meaning of "good" must transcend the categories. The uses of "good" that fall within the categories are related to each other by being connected to something that does not fall within the categories. A natural suggestion for the focal meaning of "good" is something that is completely good and not limited by being a member of one of the categories—namely, God.

As we have seen, there are good reasons to think that goodness and being are convertible. Hence, all normal uses of "good" point to something that is outside the categories and identical with being itself. The attributive account thus implies the classical conception of God as identical with being itself, goodness itself.

3.3 From Possibility[35]

Finally, it may be possible, using the resources of TMR, to provide an interesting defense for the crucial premise of one version of the ontological argument. According to that version, God's existence follows from the possibility that He exists. The argument assumes that God, if He exists, is a necessary being, and that if it is possible that necessarily p, then p. If it is possible for a necessary being to exist, then the necessary being exists.

This version of the ontological argument, known as the modal ontological argument, takes as its starting point what many, even atheists and agnostics, would readily allow: that it is at least possible that God exists. But, once unpacked, the concept of God seems to include the notions of a being that *must* exist, if He exists at all, and a being that is perfect in every way. If it really is possible that a being must exist and is perfect in every way, then said being actually exists. Once the concept of God is understood, it becomes evident that God could fail to exist only if the concept of God were somehow incoherent. Allowing the coherence and, thus, the possibility of God entails the existence of God.[36]

Of course, the crucial step in the argument is the possibility premise. What reason do we have for thinking it is possible that a necessary being exists? Philosophers have both defended and rejected this premise. What I hope to do here is offer yet another reason for thinking that the possibility premise is plausible.

If the attributive account of "good" is best understood as implying that "good" is an analogous term, then there must be a focal meaning of "good." It seems plausible to suppose that the focal meaning of "good" is something that is completely or wholly good, something that is good without limitation. That is, it is possible that there is something that is completely or wholly good. Furthermore, it is plausible to suppose that something wholly good exists in every possible world, because in every possible world "good" is analogous. So, it is possible that something is wholly good, and since what is wholly good exists in all possible worlds it follows that something wholly good exists in our world.[37]

3.4 The Fourth Way

The movement from the attributive account to the existence of God has included a number of doctrines that Aquinas, along with plenty of other medieval philosophers and theologians, held and used in a number of different ways and contexts. Such doctrines include the analogy of being, the convertibility of being and goodness, and the privation theory of evil. It would be mildly surprising if we could not use the attributive account to shed some light on the fourth way that Aquinas uses to demonstrate God's existence.

While I am no Aquinas scholar, I do know that attempting to defend, let alone explain, the fourth way is a monumental task.[38] Many Aquinas scholars have attempted to do so and, at one stage or another, have given up. It is not my intention to defend or give an explanation of the fourth way that would be acceptable to Aquinas scholars; I will not attempt to explain or defend the fourth way as Aquinas himself would, or as an Aquinas scholar desiring to be faithful to the text would. Rather, I hope to use the resources of the attributive account and some of its consequences to present a version of the fourth way that, while not pretending to be completely faithful to the text, nevertheless takes its inspiration from it.

In what follows I will present the fourth way in Aquinas's own words, give a formal presentation of it, and then represent the fourth way with a focus on just one of the items mentioned in the argument. I will then attempt to explain the relevance of the attributive account to the fourth way by drawing on some of the points already covered in this chapter.

> The fourth way is taken from the gradation to be found in things. Among beings there are some more and some less good, true, noble and the like. But "more" and "less" are predicated of different things, according as they resemble in their different ways something which is the maximum, as a thing is said to be hotter according as it more nearly resembles that which is hottest; so that there is something which is truest, something best, something noblest and, consequently, something which is uttermost being; for those things that are greatest in truth are greatest in being, as it is written in Metaph. ii. Now the maximum in any genus is the cause of all in that genus; as fire, which is the maximum heat, is the cause of all hot things. Therefore there must also be something which is to all beings the cause of their being, goodness, and every other perfection; and this we call God.[39]

The argument has the following structure:

1. Among beings there are some more and some less good, true, noble, and the like.
2. "More" and "less" are predicated of different things, according as they resemble in their different ways something that is the maximum.
3. Hence, there is something that is truest, something best, something noblest, and something that is uttermost in being.

4. The maximum in any genus is the cause of all in that genus.
5. Hence, there must be something that is to all beings the cause of their being, goodness, and every other perfection; and this we call God.

Aquinas's focus on the particular gradations of good, true, and noble is deliberate. These features are considered by him and other medievals to be convertible with each other in the way that I have argued goodness and being are convertible. Indeed, in the third premise Aquinas explicitly mentions being, thereby showing his reliance on the convertibility of being with these other perfections. While I think it worth reflecting on the convertibility of goodness, truth, and being, especially considering recent attention to various truth-maker principles and the supervenience of truth on being, doing so will take us too far afield. So, I will re-present the fourth way by focusing on just one of the items—goodness—and translating it into the attributive account.

1*. Among members of various kinds K, K^*, K^{**}, etc., some are good Ks, good K^*s, good K^{**}s, etc., and some are less good Ks, less good K^*s, less good K^{**}s, etc.
2*. "More" and "less" are predicated of different things, according as they resemble in their different ways something that is the maximum.
3*. Hence, there is something best (most good).
4*. The maximum in any genus is the cause of all in that genus.
5*. Hence, there must be something that is to all beings the cause of their goodness; and this we call God.

The idea behind the first premise is that there are degreed properties. A degreed property is a property that can be had in different degrees. Goodness is an obvious example of a degreed property. Something can be more good or less good than something else. However, we must be careful here. For, if the attributive account of "good" is correct (along with its metaphysical corollary), then goodness is not a property, but a property-marker; attributions of goodness tell us what other properties are present (depending on the K-term), and not that there is some property called "goodness" that is present. According to the attributive account, to say that x is less good than y, where x and y are members of the same kind, is to say that x has the relevant features of the kind to a degree greater than y. x is a better K than y when x exemplifies the requisite features of K-hood to a greater degree than y does.

As we saw earlier, the attributive account implies that "good" is an analogous term. The second premise in Aquinas's argument may be where the notion of analogy plays a role similar to the one it played in the first argument for God's existence presented above. This car may be better than that one; that person may be better than this one, and so on. The better-than relation makes sense when it is applied to members of the same kind. But the better-than relation also makes sense (though due to incommensurability, only sometimes) when it is applied to members of different kinds. "That person is better than that car" is not incoherent, but it does sound somewhat strained. Again, the attributive account can offer guidance. That person is better than that car, not simpliciter, but in relation to some standard, or some kind. When compared against the kind animal, the person wins every time. But even here, the comparison still seems somewhat strained. The car is not a member of the relevant kind.

According to one hypothesis, the comparisons sound strained because we are not applying the better-than relation univocally across categories. This suggests that cross-categorical comparisons involve an analogous use of the better-than relation. Cross-categorical comparisons of this sort seem to demand that we transcend the categories in the exact way spelled out above. The features that make this person better than that car are not even features that a car is supposed to have. We would not transform the car into a better one by adding to it features that the human has. So, if cross-categorical comparisons make sense, then we need to find something that unites the diverse categories, and the most plausible candidate is something outside the categories altogether.

Now once we have transcended the categories in this way, we are free to say that the thing that makes cross-categorical comparisons possible is itself the best, the maximum of each of the individual categories. If that is correct, then we have arrived at the third premise of the argument. Engaging in this type of cross-categorical comparison implies that there is something that is the maximum, not just of one category but of them all.

Before considering the second half of the fourth way argument, I would briefly like to consider a different but related path to the same conclusion we just reached. Rather than considering cases of cross-categorical comparison, let us consider cases of intra-categorical comparison. I think that we can get to the same place we just came to, but without evoking an incredulous stare that may arise from the preceding discussion of cross-categorical comparisons.

According to 2*, predication of more or less goodness requires a maximum. Aquinas' movement here is swift, and the attributive account of "good" may illuminate some of the missing moves. If x and y are both Ks, and x is a better K than y, then is there something that is the best K? Is there a best dog, a best human, a best island, etc.? It is hard to see what reason there is to suppose that when engaged in intra-categorical comparison one is committed to a best member of the kind in question. Now, one way out of this worry that neither Aquinas nor his steadfast followers are likely to endorse is to invoke the modal ontological argument once again. While intra-categorical or intra-kind comparison does not immediately entail the actual existence of a best member, it does, one might conclude, entail the possible existence of a best member. Once we transcend the categories in the ways mentioned above, it turns out that the best must be actual, if possible, for the reasons given earlier.

Another way to mollify worries about the move from intra-categorical comparison to a best member is to invoke analogy but at a different level than before. Adhering to the formalisms of the attributive account, we may re-write the second premise in the following way:

2**. If x is a less good K than y, then y resembles the best K more than x does.

2** implies there is a best K if it is possible for members of K to have varying degrees of the relevant features. But this just is the worry we have been trying to avoid. Perhaps then we need to modify 2**.

2***. If x is a less good K than y, then y resembles the best more than x does.

In other words, from intra-kind comparison, one infers that there is a something that transcends all kinds or categories. The important point to keep in mind is that the move Aquinas may be making in the second premise does not depend on the dubious notion of each kind having a best member. Instead, he may be relying on the notion that intra- or cross-categorical comparison requires the existence of something that is itself not a member of the categories. The comparisons we make within a category can be explicated in the way spelled out above: x is a better K than y just in case x has the requisite features for K-hood to a greater degree than y. But even if cross-categorical comparisons are somehow illicit, we still use the same term to describe intra-kind comparisons among different kinds. So, for example, this person may be better than that, this tree better than that, etc. But the properties that make this person better than that person are quite different from the properties that make this tree better than that tree. If we do not want to fall into semantic relativism, then good persons and good trees must be united by something other than the properties that make them good. If we attempt to locate what unifies them within one of the categories, we will have failed to explain their own kind-relative goodness. For example, we might be tempted to argue that all good Ks, K^*s, K^{**}s, etc. are unified by the abstract property of being flourishing members of their kind—or some such property.

My chief concern about the above-mentioned option is that we unite good Ks, K^*s, etc. by using to explicate their goodness a category to which many good things do not belong. If that is a false step, then the most that can be said is that good Ks, K^*s, etc. are united in their goodness, not by some property they share but by being in some way related to something good that transcends the categories. The only way to avoid this conclusion (and the same one we drew above based on cross-categorical comparisons) would be to deny cross-categorical comparisons and to embrace semantic relativism with respect to "good."[40]

I am not sure the attributive account has anything unique to offer when considering the second half of the fourth way. Aquinas moves from the existence of the best to its being the cause of everything that can be said to stand in some relation to it. The critical notion here seems to be *cause*, and getting straight on exactly what sort of causation or explanation Aquinas has in mind is crucial to assessing the plausibility of the second half of the argument.[41] However, the argument given above for the best that transcends the categories is compatible with the second half of the argument, and seems to support it quite nicely.

The fourth premise claims that the maximum in any genus is the cause of all that falls within that genus. The conclusion appears to claim that there is a cause of all being, and given the convertibility of being and goodness, a cause of all goodness. In other words, the conclusion is that there is a cause that transcends every genus, and yet is the explanation of them and their members.

This attempt to re-think the fourth way in light of the attributive account can be summarized as follows: the first part of the fourth way gets us to the best, the most good, goodness itself, which transcends all kinds or categories and every genus whatsoever. The second part gets us to the conclusion that the best, the most good, goodness itself, is the cause or explanation of everything that is good to some degree. And since being and goodness are convertible, the conclusion of the fourth way is that the best, the most good, goodness itself, is being itself, and the cause or explanation of everything that is a being.

Before concluding this section, I want to consider two objections that may have occurred to readers. According to the first objection, if we are justified in moving from good *K*s to something that is good beyond categorization, then we are justified in moving from big *K*s to something that is big beyond categorization, and we are justified in moving from small *K*s to something that is small beyond all categorization—tall, short, fat, thin, etc. But since these implications are absurd, the initial inference is problematic.

Two ways to respond to this objection are the following: First, from the fact that the inference is legitimate for one type of consideration, it does not follow that it is legitimate for other types. This restriction may be defended by an appeal to the convertibility of being and goodness. Since we have been given no reason to think that big, small, etc. are similarly convertible, we have reason to be suspicious that the inference applies to these terms. Second, the features mentioned here seem to be different from goodness in an important way. I have been arguing that the attributive account of goodness implies the existence of God. So the fact that x is a good K implies that goodness is, in some sense, related to God. But this does not imply that goodness is a purely relational property or feature. That is, the attributive account does not imply that x's goodness is not an intrinsic feature of x.[42] But the other attributives mentioned above—tall, short, fat, thin, etc.—are clearly not intrinsic features of the things that have them.

The second objection concerns God's goodness. The attributive account implies that "good" cannot logically stand alone. It does not seem that the statement "God is good" admits of an interpretation consistent with the attributive account. In the statement "God is good," there is no K term that "good" implicitly modifies. But there are at least three responses to this objection, though the responses are not necessarily jointly consistent.

First, if "good" is indeed an analogous term, it is not surprising that its focal meaning is different from its non-focal meanings (indeed this follows from the notion of analogy). The attributive account would need to be modified to exclude focal uses of "good" but doing so would not render any of the arguments in this book problematic. Rather than stating the attributive account in terms of unrestricted quantification, we would simply restrict the domain of discourse to everything except God. That is, the attributive account would apply to everything except that to which all proper uses of the term "good" point. This restriction may be defended on a number of grounds, one of which reiterates the convertibility thesis. That fact that "good" and "being" are convertible points to their transcendental nature. Terms like "good" and "being" are applicable to everything that exists and thus transcend Aristotle's categories. The attributive account supports this implication. As such, the natural home for "good" and "being" is within each of the categories but they point to something that is not categorizable. Thus, within each of the categories the attributive account is perfectly correct. But as we transcend the categories, which the attributive account implies we should, the attributive account does not make sense, not because there is something wrong with it, but simply because outside the categories our expressions lose their natural meaning and have to be understood in a different, analogous manner. It is actually a virtue of this view that the statement "God is good" does not admit of an attributive reading.

Second, the attributive account suggests that the K terms that "good" implicitly or explicitly modifies refer to things that have natures and functions. The correct metaphysical account of functions implies that something is a good instance of its kind just in case it fulfills its function to such-and-such a degree, or realizes its nature to such-and-such a degree. The same would be true of God: God is good to the extent that He fulfills

His function or realizes His nature, and thus the claim that God is good satisfies the spirit of the attributive account.

Third, it may be that a *K* term is readily available. For example, "God is good" is elliptical for "God is a good God, or God is a good deity." I am reluctant to fully endorse this response because of the Thomistic idea that God is outside of all categories and thus does not belong to a genus. Nevertheless, this response may not be incompatible with that bit of Thomism. For the claim that God is a good God may simply be a way up the ontological ladder. That is, we may think of it in the context of ancient Middle- Eastern religions, where the Hebrews are comparing the God that they worship to the gods of other peoples. In so comparing, the Hebrews may have said things like "While your god does appear good, the God we worship is actually a good, indeed the best, God." I cannot see anything wrong with such a comparison, so long as we do not move from these sorts of statements to the ontological mode; such claims do not wear their ontological significance on their sleeves.

4 Problems of Evil

I have long thought that the nature of goodness and badness is relevant both to understanding the various problems of evil and to responding to them. I am not saying that once the nature of goodness and badness are properly understood the problem of evil dissolves. Rather, I am simply claiming that the natures of goodness and badness are not irrelevant to understanding the problems and responding to it (this claim, by the way, is controversial). For example, most formulations and responses to the problems seem to assume a number of things about normativity (e.g. a utilitarian framework) and metaethics (e.g. that goods and evils can be summed) that may be false. Perhaps the problem is worse if utilitarianism is assumed, and so granting a utilitarian framework is the best way for the theist to proceed—responding to the strongest case against theism. Nevertheless, such assumptions are not innocent.

In this final section of the chapter and book, I would like briefly to explore some ideas that may help frame some of the problems that evil or badness bring vis-à-vis the existence of God and to solve (or dissolve) some of those concerns. For the most part, the theses explored and defended in this book have been tentative and partial. The same is true here, to an even greater degree.

4.1 Good and Bad Worlds

Either worlds are members of a kind or they are not.[43] If worlds are not members of a kind in the same way that dogs, humans, and birds are, then the attributive account of goodness counsels us to avoid talking about good worlds and bad worlds, and talk instead about the various things that make up a world. I think some of the work on the problem of evil by Eleonore Stump and Marilyn McCord Adams is a move in this direction.[44] These writers think that there is something wrong with examining, for example, the badness of World War II as something over and above the badness of this and that individual act or individual life, etc. The badness of the war is nothing over and above the badness of these lives and acts—the badness of the evil suffered and evil done. One way to motivate this focus is by appealing to the attributive account of goodness and badness.

As we have seen, the attributive account suggests that to say that x is good is either to say that x is a good K or to say nothing at all, at least when we are dealing with denizens of this world. Typically x will have a nature or function. If we are dealing with something that does not have a nature or function, calling it either good or bad will seem out of place. The attributive account explains why "x is a good rock" and "x is a good sunset" sound odd. In Chapter 4 we noted that there are occasions when such claims are legitimate, and by appealing to a modified form of Koons's normative theory of function we were able to accommodate such uses within an attributive framework. The same story might be told regarding claims like "x is a good (or bad) war," and "x is a good (or bad) world." Such claims are more like "x is a good rock," and "x is a good pile of leaves" than "x is a good person" or "x is a good pen." Thus, we should not, when considering the problem (or problems) of evil think about the badness or goodness, first and foremost, of some war or world, precisely because these are not things with a nature or function.

But suppose that this world is a member of some kind in the way that scientific essentialists claim. Then saying of our world that it is good or bad will be perfectly acceptable on the attributive account. Just as the goodness or badness of a human must depend on the nature of a human, the goodness or badness of a world will depend on the nature of a world. It may be that there are different kinds of worlds, just as there are different kinds of animals. Our world is member of one kind of world, and some other world is a member of some other kind of world. Or it may be that there are not different kinds of worlds in a way similar to there not being different kinds of humans. Either way, I think we can get some traction on the problem of good and bad worlds by considering what a world is and what features worlds can and should have.

At a minimum, a world must be something complete or exhaustive in some way. It is complete in the sense that for every proposition p, either p or its negation is true, or that for every state of affairs, either it or its negation obtains, or. . . . Something along those lines is necessary and maybe sufficient for a thing to count as a world in the first place. Given the convertibility of being and goodness, and assuming that worlds are something over and above their members, worlds will be good qua worlds. But the attributive account of badness suggests it will not make sense to say that some world is a bad one, unless it makes sense to say that it is both a world and that it is lacking some feature worlds are supposed to have. If it makes no sense to think of features worlds are supposed to have in virtue of their membership in world-kind, then it will not make sense to think of bad worlds.

I am sure that there are many candidate features that will come to mind as to which worlds should have qua worlds. But because I am simply attempting to explore this area, let me suggest one feature that worlds should have, from the Christian point of view. Worlds are supposed to express the glory of God in ways that perhaps only worlds can. Just as humans and trees express the glory of God in related but different ways, if worlds really are members of kinds, then they too should express God's glory in some way. Having to glorify God in a unique way may have the interesting consequence that, as in the human and tree case, we will not be able to tell whether this world expresses God's glory in its own way until the end of the world, or until it reaches maturation. Until then we can perhaps justifiably assert that the world appears to be expressing God's glory in this way as opposed to that, but such judgments should be as tempered in the world case as they should be in the human case.

4.2 Privation, Convertibility, the Attributive Account, and the Problem of Evil

According to the privation theory of evil, evil (or badness in general) is the absence of some good that is supposed to be present. I want to draw two interesting consequences that appear to follow from the privation account of evil, the attributive account of goodness, and the convertibility of being and goodness: (a) there cannot be more evil than goodness, and (b) goodness is explanatorily prior to evil.

In defense of (a), it is important to recall that according to the privation theory of evil, evil is not a thing. Evil has no being qua evil, and for something to be evil there must be some being that exists that lacks some feature it ought to have. Given the convertibility of being and goodness, we know that goodness is something. Furthermore, given the attributive account of goodness, we know that the goodness of a thing is determined by the kind of thing it is. The kind of thing something is circumscribes the kind and amount of goodness it can have.

The same is true of evil. The kind of thing something is circumscribes the kind and amount of badness it can have. I can be a bad human, but not a bad tree. The convertibility thesis allows us to say that, qua human, I have all the goodness that a thing has in virtue of being a human. I cannot cease to have that kind and amount of goodness without ceasing to be human. And because I am bad to whatever extent I fail to actualize those features that humans should have (or fail to actualize those features that humans should have at my stage in human development), it seems that the extent to which I am bad cannot exceed the extent to which I am good. Being a bad human implies being a human, which implies being good qua human, which implies having the kind and amount of goodness that membership in the human-kind guarantees. Being a bad human implies failing to have one or more of those features that humans should have in virtue of being human. But that kind of badness is parasitic on human goodness, and seemingly cannot exceed the kind of goodness that is identical with being a human. Of course, the same can be said *mutatis mutandis* of every kind of goodness and badness possible.[45] Hence, there cannot be more evil than goodness.

Another argument in favor of (a) starts with one of the clarifications to the privation theory of evil that I made earlier in this chapter. I argued that the privation theory is best thought of as the claim that evil is the absence of some *feature* that should be present in some substance. The missing entity that explains the badness is, thus, at the ontological level of a feature and not at the level of a substance. If we are willing to accept the idea that features are lower on the ontological ladder than substances, then the claim that there cannot be more badness than goodness follows. "x is a bad K" amounts to x, a substance, lacking some feature. Since, according to the great chain of being, features have less being than substances, the goodness of x is greater than the absent feature that accounts for x's badness. Thus, from the privation theory itself, together with something like the great chain of being, (a) follows.

Obviously, more work is needed to make this argument more compelling, but there seems to me to be something right about it. For any instance of evil you care to mention, there must be at least as much goodness to support that instance of evil. (a) may be true independently of the attributive account, but I think the attributive account lends considerable support to it.

In defense of (b) consider the following: if x is both ontologically and epistemically more fundamental than y, then x is explanatorily prior to y. It seems that given the privation theory of evil, the convertibility thesis and the attributive account of goodness, it follows that goodness is both ontologically and epistemically more fundamental than badness. One reason for thinking that goodness is ontologically more fundamental than badness is that since badness is not a thing, but a lack of a specific sort, badness is parasitic on goodness, and thus goodness is ontologically more basic.

One reason for thinking that goodness is epistemically more basic than badness is that knowing that x is a bad K assumes knowing that x is not as it is supposed to be, which assumes knowing, perhaps implicitly or partially, what x is supposed to be, which assumes knowing what a good x is. Hence, knowing that x is a bad K assumes knowing what a good K is. Hence, goodness is epistemically prior to badness.

Another reason for thinking that goodness is epistemically more basic than badness comes from the privation theory of evil. It is plausible to suppose that absences are less basic epistemically than the things that are lacking. Put differently, it is plausible to suppose that negative states of affairs are less basic epistemically than positive states of affairs. Privations are epistemically less fundamental than positives. If that is right, and the privation theory of evil is true, then badness is epistemically less basic than goodness.

If it true that goodness is explanatorily prior to badness, the theist can legitimately ask the non-theist for an explanation of goodness without compunction. According to one of the premises in a version of the argument from evil, the probability of God's existence given the amount and kinds of evil in our world is low. But since goodness is explanatorily prior to evil, it seems that the theist can refuse to accept this premise and instead suggest the following: the probability of God's existence given the amount and kinds of goodness in this world is high. If that is right and the privation theory is right, then the premise cited above in the argument from evil cannot be true. It cannot be true, because the amount and kinds of evil in our world entail certain things about the amount and kinds of goodness in our world, which, in turn, imply that God, the supreme good, goodness itself, exists.

It is time to bring this chapter and book to a close. Since P. T. Geach has played a prominent role in this book it is fitting to conclude with a quote from him that has clear application to the study undertaken here:

> I am well aware that much of this discussion is unsatisfying: some points on which I think I do see clear I have not been able to develop at proper length; on many points I certainly do not see clear. But perhaps, though I have not made everything clear, I have made some things clearer.[46]

Notes

Introduction

1 George Von Wright, *The Varieties of Goodness* (London: Routledge, 1964).
2 Peter Geach, "Good and Evil," in *20th Century Ethical Theory*, ed. Steven M. Cahn and Joram G. Haber (Upper Saddle River, NJ: Prentice Hall, 1995), 300–6.
3 Rosalind Hursthouse, *On Virtue Ethics* (Oxford: Oxford University Press, 1999), 195.
4 Philippa Foot, *Natural Goodness* (Oxford: Oxford University Press, 2001), 3.
5 See Chapter 4.
6 David J. Buller, "Etiological Theories of Function: A Geographical Survey," *Biology and Philosophy* 13 (1998): 520.
7 Denis Walsh, "Evolutionary Essentialism," *British Journal for the Philosophy of Science* 57 (2006): 426.
8 Judith Jarvis Thomson certainly agrees with that.
9 For expression of the worry that Geach's account implies that there is no such thing as intrinsic value see Michael Zimmerman's, "In Defense of the Concept of Intrinsic Value," *Canaadian Journal of Philosophy* 29 (1999): 389–410 and *The Nature of Intrinsic Value* (Lanham: Rowman & Littlefield Publishers, Inc., 2001).

Chapter 1 : Contemporary Moral Realism: Problems with a Common Assumption

1 My main purpose in this chapter is to motivate a new version of moral realism by showing that current versions are not plausible as they stand. Thus, attention is focused on two of the most popular versions of moral realism and not on each and every version. However, the arguments presented in this chapter, as well as in Chapters 2 and 3 can be extended *mutatis mutandis* to other versions of moral realism not discussed here.
2 David Copp, introduction to *Oxford Handbook of Ethical Theory*, ed. David Copp (Oxford: Oxford University Press, 2006), 8.
3 Copp, *Oxford Handbook of Ethical Theory*, 4n.

4 Since, I know of no recent attempt to develop a version of moral realism that appeals to synthetic a priori identity claims, the division between analytic and synthetic identities is the same as the division between identities discoverable a priori and those discoverable a posteriori.
5 Geoffrey Sayre-McCord, "Moral Realism," in *Oxford Handbook of Ethical Theory*, ed. David Copp (Oxford: Oxford University Press, 2006), 40.
6 Sayre-McCord, "Moral Realism," 44.
7 Saul Kripke, *Naming and Necessity* (Cambridge: Harvard University Press, 1980).
8 Sayre-McCord, "Moral Realism," 50.
9 Since Mooreanism with its commitment to *sui generis* moral properties is currently a minority position (though perhaps a growing minority) I will not consider it. See Russ Shafer-Landau *Moral Realism: A Defense* (Oxford: Oxford University Press, 2003) for a contemporary version and defense of Mooreanism. It is important to note however that Shafer-Landau's version of Mooreanism continues to make use of the assumption that goodness is a monadic property capable of figuring into synthetic property identities. The main difference between Shafer-Landau's version of moral realism and other versions is that Shafer-Landau argues that goodness is constituted by natural properties and not identical with them. Note also that Shafer-Landau's attempt to resurrect a kind of Mooreanism is motivated by similar concerns expressed here. In particular Shafer-Landau finds fault with contemporary accounts of moral realism and attempts to develop his own account free from the defects he finds in others.
10 I leave off Moore's third disjunct, namely "'good' is meaningless" in order to keep things relatively simple and because adding it does nothing to change the purpose of the chapter.
11 The main objections to non-natural moral realism are epistemological and metaphysical. Since I do not discuss non-natural moral realism in this book, I will not present the main objections to it. However, in Chapter 2 I do present some semantic reasons for believing that Moore's version of non-natural moral realism fails.
12 Saul Kripke, *Naming and Necessity*. Hilary Putnam, "The Meaning of 'Meaning'," in *Mind, Language and Reality, Philosophical Papers* 2, 215–71. (Cambridge: Cambridge University Press, 1979).
13 Richard Boyd, "How to Be a Moral Realist," in *Essays on Moral Realism*, ed. Geoffrey Sayre-McCord (Ithaca: Cornell University Press, 1988), 181–228.
14 By arguing that synthetic moral naturalism fails, I am in agreement with Terence Horgan and Mark Timmons who argue for the same conclusion in a series of papers. "New Wave Moral Realism Meets Moral Twin Earth," *Journal of Philosophical Research* 16 (1990–91): 447–65; "Troubles on Moral Twin Earth: Moral Queerness Revived," *Synthese*

92 (1992): 221–60; "Troubles for New Wave Moral Semantics: The 'Open Question Argument' Revived," *Philosophical Papers* 21 (1992): 153–75; "From Moral Realism to Moral Relativism in One Easy Step," *Critica* 28 (1996): 3–39; "Copping Out on Moral Twin Earth," *Synthese* 124 (2000): 139–52. However, my arguments for the same conclusion are, as far as I can tell, completely independent of theirs. Thus, if their arguments fail (which a number of philosophers have suggested), mine may still do the trick.

15 Not to mention Moore's conclusion has been grist for the anti-realists' mill.
16 Boyd, "How to Be a Moral Realist," 195.
17 The distinction between weak and strong rigid designators is not important for the purposes of this chapter.
18 Kripke, *Naming and Necessity*, 121.
19 CSN is from Horgan and Timmons, "Troubles for New Wave Moral Semantics," 159.
20 Horgan and Timmons (H&T) argue that accounts, such as Boyd's, are false, but for different reasons than the one's offered here. H&T attempt to show that a posteriori ethical naturalists, such as Boyd, face the following dilemma: either the reference-fixing relation R is too indeterminate to pick out a unique natural property (or relation) that satisfies one and only one normative theory, or R does pick out a unique natural property that satisfies one and only one normative theory at the expense of implying some version of relativism that is incompatible with ethical naturalism. The first horn of the dilemma claims that, for example, R is satisfied by natural properties that satisfy both consequentialism and deontologism. The second horn of the dilemma takes us to Moral Twin Earth ("Copping out on Moral Twin Earth," 140). The inhabitants of Moral Twin Earth use "right" in much the same way that inhabitants of earth use the term "right." Further, the reference-fixing relation on Moral Twin Earth picks out a unique property that satisfies one and only one normative theory. R on earth fixes the referent of a natural property that uniquely satisfies consequentialism, whereas, on Moral Twin Earth, R fixes the referent of a different natural property that uniquely satisfies deontologism. If difference of referent implies difference in meaning, then earthers and twin-earthers do not mean the same thing when talking about right actions. Thus, there is no moral disagreement between earthlings and twin-earthlings. They are simply talking past each other. H&T call this outcome chauvinistic conceptual relativism. If difference of referent does not imply difference in meaning, then the "very same moral judgment may . . . be true for earthlings and false for twin earthlings" ("Copping out on Moral Twin Earth," 141). H&T call this outcome standard relativism. Notice that both chauvinistic moral relativism and standard relativism imply that earthlings and

twin-earthlings do not engage in moral disagreements. This, according to H&T, is contrary to our linguistic intuitions. Thus, a posteriori ethical naturalism is false. See footnote 13 for additional references.

21 See Torin Alter and Russell Daw, "Free Acts and Robot Cats," *Philosophical Studies* 102 (2001): 345–57. Alter and Daw construct a similar argument directed toward a different target.

22 See Michael Devitt and Kim Sterelny, *Language and Reality*, 2nd edn. (Cambridge, MA: MIT Press, 1999).

23 Perhaps S must have the description ". . . is a species" in mind. This seems doubtful. As Richard Miller points out, it shouldn't be necessary to have ". . . is a species" in mind in order to successfully refer to tigers qua tigers. Surely the initial baptizer could be ignorant about the difference between species and genera and nevertheless succeed in referring to tigers. It may be that there just is not a plausible solution to the qua-problem that is not committed to a robust form of descriptivism. If that is correct, then so much the worse for Boyd's account of moral naturalism. See Richard Miller, "A Purely Causal Solution to One of the Qua-Problems for the Causal Theory of Reference," *Australasian Journal of Philosophy* 70 (1992): 425–34.

24 A priori in the sense that a competent user of the term could come to recognize the descriptions as being true.

25 For example, red falls under the determinable color, and tigers are members of the cat genus.

26 Note that in the case of tigers and the description ". . . is a species" used to ground reference, it is plausible to suppose that whatever kinds species fall under, tigers fall under them as well.

27 Of course both of these are in fact philosophically contentious. James Griffin raises some interesting worries about moral supervenience in *Well-Being: Its Meaning, Measurement, and Moral Importance* (Oxford: Clarendon Press, 1986). I raise some concerns about moral supervenience in "Problems with Moral/Natural Supervenience," *Religious Studies* 47 (2011): 73–84. The action-guidingness of evaluative utterances is questioned by judgment externalists.

28 Again, see Alter and Daw "Free Acts and Robot Cats," for a similar argument regarding a different topic.

29 If you do not like my examples of non-moral goodness, I believe it will not take much effort to supply your own.

30 I am assuming for the sake of argument that there is such a thing as the property of goodness and the property of non-moral goodness. Indeed, I am assuming for the sake of argument that we understand the difference between moral and non-moral goodness.

31 Another response to the moral qua-problem is to take the initial baptism of N with "good" as not differentiating between moral and non-moral goodness. That is, S baptizes N with good and S intends to baptize all

and only morally and non-morally good things. The problem here is that *S*'s baptism is clearly *not* a baptism of a natural kind with a natural essence. If it is not, then synthetic moral naturalism is implausible from the start.

32 Robert Adams, *Finite and Infinite Goods: A Framework for Ethics* (Oxford: Oxford University Press, 1999).

33 Linda Zagzebski's recent book *Divine Motivation Theory* (Cambridge: Cambridge University Press, 2004) is, like Adams's, full of insight and wisdom. Nevertheless, like Adams, her attempt to appropriate KP developments seems to me to fail. One of the problems that confronts Zagzebski's attempt to employ KP developments is similar to a problem we have already seen. Suppose that it is true that we pick out the practically wise person not by first having a description of practical wisdom in mind, but by simple ostentation. Thus, some use Gandhi as the exemplar while others use Jesus or Mohammed. But these figures also radically differ. In order to ensure that the thing we are talking about with respect to Gandhi is the same thing we are talking about with respect to Jesus or Mohammed, we will need some sort of description; otherwise the respective communities will not be talking about the same thing. Zagzebski mentions that a similarity condition with be needed, and I suspect that the similarity condition is meant to handle this worry. But if that is right, then either the similarity condition will include some sort of descriptive content or it will not. If it does, then Zagzebski's attempt to employ some of the resources provided by direct reference theory do not do the job she claims they do. If it does not, then we are left with the kind of relativism incompatible with moral realism.

34 Adams, *Finite and Infinite Goods*, 13.
35 Ibid., 14.
36 Ibid., 15.
37 Ibid.
38 As we have also seen the qua-problem puts significant pressure on this point.
39 Adams, *Finite and Infinite Goods*, 16.
40 Ibid.
41 Ibid.
42 Ibid.
43 Note that Adams's replacement for the causal theory looks strikingly similar to a full blown descriptivism. Aristotle is whoever satisfies all or most or many of the definite descriptions. Similarly, good is whatever satisfies all or most or many of the roles revealed by our use of the term "good." If this is right and Adams replaces (3) with descriptivism, then there is no way for him to support (1) and (2). The nature of a thing will be its nominal essence. In Section 3.2, I will elaborate on this concern.
44 Adams, *Finite and Infinite Goods*, 17.

45 Ibid., 18.
46 Ibid., 19.
47 Ibid.
48 Ibid., 20.
49 Ibid., 28.
50 Ibid., 42.
51 Ibid.
52 Ibid., 16.
53 Robert Stalnaker, "Reference and Necessity," in *Blackwell Companions to Philosophy: A Companion to the Philosophy of Language*, ed. Bob Hale and Crispin Wright (Oxford: Wiley-Blackwell 1999), 536.
54 Adams, *Finite and Infinite Goods*, 24. I doubt that the reason for selecting H_2O as the nature of water and not some complex structural or disjunctive property is that H_2O is merely the better explanation. Earthlings' causal contact is with H_2O and not XYZ. Given the causal theory of reference, Earthlings use of the term 'water' is causally related not to XYZ but to H_2O. This is important for Putnam's argument for semantic externalism. What is causally responsible for our use of a term, according to Putnam, is, in some cases, the meaning of that term. Semantic externalism thus requires CTR and not a best candidate theory.
55 Or the fact that two different things appear to satisfy the roles may lead us to suspect that the roles reveal that the referent is not a natural kind at all.
56 I take this to be the natural reading of Adams's account. While it is true that Adams modifies the KP way of distinguishing between semantics and metaphysics Adams's modification is meant to be a generalization of the KP account and not incompatible with it. Furthermore, it is worth noting that Adams's modification is only to the third element of the Kripke/Putnam account and not, as far as I can tell, to either of the first two. Thus, I contend my reading is the natural one.
57 Adams, *Finite and Infinite Goods*, 15.
58 Ibid., 28.
59 Ibid., 42–3.
60 Adams notes that Iris Murdoch also suggests something very similar.
61 Adams, *Finite and Infinite Goods*, 44.
62 This version of the objection has been presented to me independently by Robert Koons, John Hare, and C. Stephen Evans. I am grateful to each for their help throughout.

Chapter 2: Geach's Claim: Explication and Defense

1 P. T. Geach, *Analysis*, 17 (1956): 32–42. Subsequent references will be to the antholgized version found in *20th Century Ethical Theory*, ed. Steven Cahn and Joram Haber (New Jersey: Prentice Hall, 1995), 300–6.

2 "*x* is an *A N*," where A is attributive, is supposed to represent (or begin to represent) the logical form or deep structure of sentences containing attributive adjectives. Thus, a sentence of the form "*x* is *A*" is elliptical for "*x* is an *A N*."

3 I have adapted these from Mark Sainsbury, *Logical Forms: An Introduction to Philosophical Logic* (Oxford: Blackwell, 1991), 149.

4 Objection: From "John is a good chemist" and "all chemists are scientists" we may infer that "John is a good scientist." Reply: Consider a world W in which all and only chemists are physicists. Hence, in W all the scientists are chemists and physicists. John is a scientist. Hence, John is a chemist and a physicist. However, John is a good chemist but a bad physicist. Does it follow that John is a good scientist? I do not think it does. Even if I am wrong about this sort of example there is another kind of example in the neighborhood that does seem to work. From "*x* is a good scientist" and "*x* is a chemist" it does not follow that "*x* is a good chemist." *x* may be an average chemist but a superb physicist. However, from "*x* is a red vehicle" and "*x* is a bike" it does follow that *x* is a red bike even if *x* also happens to be an airplane (think of James Bond-like contraptions). See below for more discussion.

5 Geach, "Good and Evil," 301. This does not follow, but it is how Geach seems to move in the text.

6 This second reason is what distinguishes *alienans* adjectives from other attributives. *Alienans* adjectives alienate the noun they modify from its normal role.

7 It's beside the point in the sense that not passing the splitting test is sufficient for inclusion in the attributive adjective class. The fact that "bad" is more like an *alienans* than "good" is relevant to other considerations, such as the differences between badness and goodness. I will not explore these differences here but I will note that the fact that "bad" satisfies both features mentioned above strongly suggests that something like a privation theory of evil is implied. A bad *K* lacks properties or degrees of properties that a *K* and a good *K* possess. Also, notice that the following equivalence seems true: The privation theory is true if, and only if, the convertibility of goodness and being is true. If the equivalence holds, then Geach's claim that "good" and "bad" are essentially attributive has quite interesting implications hitherto unnoticed. I explore some of these themes in the last section of Chapter 5.

8 The move from "*x* is a good N" to "*x* is a good K" is deliberate. I will explain the motivation below.

9 See Paul H. Portner, *What is Meaning?: Fundamentals of Formal Semantics* (Blackwell: Oxford, 2005).

10 Geach, "Good and Evil," 304.

11 Objection: nothing in the logic of "good" or "bad" suggests that the modified has to have a function. Thus, the logic of good permits statements like "*x* is a good pebble" or "*x* is a good corpse." Reply: First

things first. The logic of "good" does not entail the claim that the modified must have a function or essence. But it is rather curious that "good pebble" and "good corpse" sound odd. Nevertheless, from the logic plus some other premises we can get to the conclusion that the modified must have a function or essence. The remaining chapters will attempt to provide the missing links. For now, I will simply assume that the modified must have a function or nature.
12 The addition of nature will be explained in the chapters to follow.
13 Peter T. Geach, *The Virtues* (Cambridge: Cambridge University Press, 1971), Chapters 1 and 5.
14 The phrase "nature or function" can at this early stage be understood to mean one or the other or both. The next chapter will argue that natures determine functions in some cases and functions determine nature in other cases. Something may have functions in a secondary sense, but these too will be related to the nature of the thing insofar as the nature has properties that are either accidental or non-essential necessities. For example, the nature of a book determines its function. The nature of a book includes its being a written work in some language intended for an audience. A book may also be used for a doorstop. A book's having the function of being able to be used as a doorstop is accidental to its nature in the sense that in order to be a book it need not be even capable of being a doorstop—for example, an e-book.
15 Geach actually employs a number of arguments against the predicative use of "good" in "Good and Evil." The argument proper is the one that is central to this chapter. The others will be brought to bear in defending the argument proper. I assume that this was Geach's intention all along, contrary to what Charles Pigden seems to imply in "Geach on Good," *The Philosophical Quarterly* 40 (159) (1990): 129–54. See below for a discussion of Pigden's objection to the argument proper.
16 Geach's claim: necessarily, for all x, if x is good then x is a good K. The first type of objection claims: there is an x such that x is good and x is not a good K and there is an x such that x is good and x is a good K.
17 In Chapter 5 I will take up an objection to the semantic unity claim.
18 Obviously this style of argument will not work against those who claim that good is always something other than attributive.
19 This amounts to the following: it is not the case that there is an x such that x is good and x is a good K.
20 Objectivism is Geach's term for G. E. Moore's metaethical theory.
21 G. E. Moore, *Principia Ethica* (Amherst: Prometheus Books, 1988): iiiv–ix.
22 Moore, *Principia Ethica*, x.
23 Ibid., 2.
24 Alfred F. MacKay, "Attributive-Predicative," *Analysis* 30 (March 1970): 113–20.

25 MacKay, "Attributive-Predicative," 116–17.
26 Ibid., 117.
27 Geach, "Good and Evil," 301.
28 Pigden, "Geach on Good."
29 Ibid., 131.
30 Ibid., 131–2.
31 Think also of malaria and the aids virus. While these seem to be uniformly bad for humans it is also possible to assess malaria and aids in terms of their functioning.
32 Or sickle cell may be good for humans infected with malaria.
33 The two accounts of kind-interaction outlined in the text are similar to what Brian Davies and Herbert McCabe attribute to Aquinas. See Brian Davies, *The Thought of Thomas Aquinas* (Oxford: Oxford University Press, 1992); Herbert McCabe, *God Matters* (London: Geoffrey Chapman, 1987). I discovered this similarity after formulating the two accounts.
34 Lynne Rudder-Baker, "The Ontology of Artifacts," *Philosophical Explorations* 7 (2) (2004): 99–111. Rudder-Baker has an interesting discussion of the nature of artifacts and artifactual malfunction. In Chapters 3 and 4 I return to artifacts and actions and argue that the nature of humans and intentions must be brought to bear on artifactual and action evaluation.
35 In Chapter 5 I will return to this worry, and argue that one way to overcome it is to argue that "good" is an analogical term. I will then use the idea of "good" being analogical to develop a few different arguments for God's existence.
36 Geach, "Good and Evil," 303.
37 In Chapter 5 I will discuss a different but related worry.
38 In Chapter 3 I attempt to elaborate on this.
39 The "for the most part" qualification is obviously important. Thomson does not think that the function of humans is relevant for determining what a good human is. Apart from humans, Thomson does appear ready to endorse the claim that the function of a thing is relevant to determining its goodness.
40 Judith Thomson, "The Right and the Good," *The Journal of Philosophy* 94 (2) (1997): 278.
41 By requiring success in order for an act to possess a virtue property Thomson seems to be committing herself to some sort of virtue-consequentialism.
42 Thomson distinguishes between goodness-for and "on balance goodness-for" and argues that the former and not the latter is what is needed in order for some act to possess a virtue property.
43 Thomson, "The Right and the Good," 288.
44 Ibid., 289.

45 Ibid., 278.
46 The first reconstruction of Thomson's objection amounts to the claim $(\exists x)(x$ is good and x is not a good $K)$. The second reconstruction of Thomson's objection, which takes into consideration her claim that Geach's story, like Moore's, is incomplete, amounts to the claim $\sim(\exists x)(x$ is good and x is a good $K)$. The first is of course compatible with $(\exists x)(x$ is good and x is a good $K)$; the second is not compatible with this.
47 Thomson, "The Right and the Good," 289.
48 Indeed a bad member of the latter kind may also benefit the former kind. For example, an extremely dull knife may help to flatten the cake whereas a perfectly sharp knife may cause dents in the surface.
49 Michael Zimmerman, "In Defense of the Concept of Intrinsic Value," *Canaadian Journal of Philosophy* 29 (1999): 389–410; *The Nature of Intrinsic Value* (Lanham: Rowman & Littlefield Publishers, Inc., 2001): 15.
50 This same point regarding the context-dependency of all adjectives is made quite clearly and forcefully by Ran Lahav, "Against Compositionality: the case of adjectives," *Philosophical Studies* 57 (3) (1989): 261–79.
51 Zimmerman, *The Nature of Intrinsic Value*, 14.
52 Ibid., 15.
53 Zimmerman does not explicitly state the upshot, but it is clear that this is what Zimmerman has in mind. Nor does Zimmerman refer to what I have called the higher-order and lower-order test. Nevertheless, for Zimmerman's objection to stick it must be the case that most adjectives fail *both* tests.

Chapter 3: Some Metaethical Implications of the Attributive Account of "Good"

1 In Chapter 5 I will consider two other metaethical implications of the attributive account, namely, that goodness and being are identical, and the privation theory of evil.
2 More precisely, "good" is a predicate-forming functor that takes kind-terms as arguments and yields predicates that refer to magnitudes of properties. Since I will be assuming throughout that there is a metaphysical corollary of the attributive account of "good," I will often eliminate reference to terms and predicates and simply speak of their referents. I realize that it is a large assumption to think that there is a metaphysical corollary of the attributive account, but it would likely require a book-length treatment to defend it. At the very least the attributive account, if correct, provides some evidence for its corresponding metaphysical thesis.
3 Such-and-such a degree is meant to be shorthand for what degree is required for something to be a good instance of its kind.

4 This example is taken from Zoltan Gendler Szabo's, "Adjectives in Context," in *Perspectives on Semantics, Pragmatics, and Discourse*, ed. Istvan Kenesei and Robert M. Harnish (Amsterdam: John Benjamins Publishing Company, 2001), 119–45. It should be noted that Szabo uses the example to refute the attributive account, whereas I think that the example actually helps show the plausibility of the attributive account.
5 Saul Kripke, "Identity and Necessity," in *Metaphysics: The Big Questions*, ed. Peter van Inwagen and Dean W. Zimmerman (Malden: Blackwell Publishing, 2008), 532.
6 I discovered Soames' expression of this point after I had made the same discovery (if it is one).
7 Scott Soames, "Kripke on Epistemic and Metaphysical Possibility: Two Routes to the Necessary Aposteriori," in *Saul Kripke*, ed. Alan Berger (Cambridge: Cambridge University Press, 2010), 78–99.
8 Michael Tye, "Mental states, Adverbial Theory of," in *Routledge Encyclopedia of Philosophy*, ed. E. Craig (London: Routledge, 1998).
9 Michael Loux, "Toward an Aristotelian Theory of Abstract Objects," *Midwest Studies in Philosophy: Studies in Essentialism* 11 (1986): 498.
10 Ibid.
11 Ibid.
12 In Chapter 5 I will argue that the attributive account implies that being and goodness are convertible with each other. That may appear to conflict with the claim that only things with a nature or functions can be good. The conflict is only apparent. First, the extension of beings and things with a nature or function are the same. Second, as will be noted in Chapter 4, the class of things with natures or functions is quite broad and will include things that do not seem to have either a function or a nature. Analysis will reveal that such items can be seen to have a function or nature within context. Third, and related to the second point, Loux's attempt to eliminate or reduce non-substances to substances and their modifications will, if successful, likely eliminate all concerns about the compatibility between the claim argued here and the convertibility claim argued in Chapter 5.
13 What about rocks and corpses? It seems that a rock or corpse could in some sense be a functioning member of the kind it belongs to, but that it is not appropriate to call either rocks or corpses good. In this case, only one direction of the biconditional is satisfied. Hence, these examples are not counterexamples to the biconditional. In the next chapter I will consider contexts where it is appropriate to say "that's a good rock" or "that's a good corpse." As we will see, contexts where it is appropriate to call a rock or a corpse good actually enhance the plausibility of the present account by referring to an implicit function.
14 The distinction between primary and non-primary kind is important here because I am claiming that a thing's nature and/or function establishes evaluative criteria (or helps to determine whether or not it is good).

15 Kit Fine, "Essence and Modality," *Philosophical Perspectives* 8 (1994): 1–16.
16 Assuming, of course, that sets exist.
17 I have replaced Rea's term "dominant" with "primary."
18 Michael Rea, "In Defense of Mereological Universalism," *Philosophy and Phenomenological Research* 58 (2) (1998): 358.
19 This example is taken from Thomson's "The Right and the Good," 291.
20 I assume throughout that artifacts have natures and thus really exist. This assumption has been denied most recently by Peter van Inwagen, David Lewis, and Trenton Merricks. Nothing crucial to my account hangs on the ontological status of artifacts, so I will not attempt to defend the assumption here. See Peter van Inwagen, *Material Beings* (Ithaca, NY: Cornell University Press, 1990); David Lewis, *Parts of Classes* (Oxford: Basil Blackwell, 1991); Trenton Merricks, *Objects and Persons* (Oxford: Clarendon Press, 2001). For defenses of the claim that artifacts really exist see Amie Thomasson, "Realism and Human Kinds," *Philosophy and Phenomenological Research* 67 (3) 2003: 580–609; Lynne Rudder-Baker, "The Ontology of Artifacts," *Philosophical Explorations* 7 (2) (2004): 99–111.
21 I suspect that the relationship between natures and functions with respect to non-human animals and plants is one of necessary co-extension. If one takes necessary co-extension to imply identity, then the relationship between functions and natures in the non-animal and plant cases will be the same as the relationship between functions and natures in the artifactual cases.
22 Recall the discussion in Chapter 2 about *alienans* adjectives. One of the features *alienans* adjectives highlighted in that earlier discussion was that if A is an *alienans* adjective, then in statements where A modifies N, what is normally true of an N minus A will not necessarily be true of an N plus A. "Artificial" is an *alienans* adjective. Thus, what is normally true of hearts is not necessarily true of artificial hearts.
23 This is but one difference among many between artifacts and natural kinds. See Amie Thomasson, "Artifacts and Human Concepts," in *Creations of the Mind: Essays on Artifacts and their Representation*, ed. Stephen Laurence and Eric Margolis (Oxford: Oxford University Press, 2007).
24 Another way to see the connection between goodness and function is by considering cases where a thing's function and nature are completely unknown. In such cases, it seems impossible to assert with any assurance either that the thing is good or bad or that doing such-and-such to it would be good or bad. Cases like these strike me as providing reasons to support the claim that things without functions and natures simply cannot be good. This is, of course, true even if the set of things without natures or functions is empty.

25 Thomson, "The Right and the Good." See also, R. M. Hare, "Geach: Good and Evil," *Analysis* 18 (1957): 103–12.
26 See Jyl Gertzler, "The Attractions and Delights of Goodness," *The Philosophical Quarterly* 54 (216) (2003): 361.
27 Gertzler, "The Attractions and Delights of Goodness," 361.
28 Interestingly, Brian Davies seems to suggest something similar in the case of divine goodness. Since God cannot fail to fully realize his nature and function God cannot fail to be good. Thus, calling God good is (in the sense we are considering) redundant. See Brian Davies, *The Thought of Thomas Aquinas* (New York: Oxford University Press, 1993).
29 Since the topic of human goodness is large I save a discussion of this example for the next section.
30 See Linda Zagzebski, *Divine Motivation Theory* (Cambridge: Cambridge University Press, 2004), 272–3. Zagzebski's discussion is influenced by a similar point made by Stuart Hampshire. See Stuart Hampshire, "Ethics: A Defense of Aristotle," in *Freedom of Mind and Other Essays*, ed. Stuart Hampshire (Princeton: Princeton University Press, 1971).
31 Notice that the response I gave to the good pebble/good corpse objection may apply to the good sunset objection as well. If sunsets are not genuine things, then they are barred from occupying the argument position in the predicate-forming functor "good."
32 If it is clear that the claim "that's good news" is not elliptical, then the only way to evaluate the claim would be by considering the function of news qua news.
33 Throughout this section I assume that if John is a human, then John's primary kind is human. Furthermore, I assume (though I do provide some reasons for believing) that the goodness that is determined by a thing's primary kind has more weight than the goodness determined by a thing's non-primary kinds, in the following sense: if John is a human and a teacher, then in any situations where the evaluative standards determined by the nature of being a teacher conflict with the evaluative standards determined by the nature of being a human (assuming there are some), the evaluative standards determined by the nature of being a human outweigh the evaluative standards determined by the nature of being a teacher. For a defense of the basic strategy here (though with a kind of non-realist perspective) see Christine M Korsgaard, *The Sources of Normativity* (Cambridge: Cambridge University Press, 1996).
34 For example, Thomson's "The Right and the Good" as well as her more recent *Goodness and Advice* (Princeton: Princeton University Press, 2001). Each can be read as being partially motivated by a concern to avoid this implication.
35 It is important to remember that by "kind" I do not privilege natural kinds over others (e.g. artifactual).

36 Perhaps pebbles and corpses lack natures and functions. If so, then that would help to explain why talk of good pebbles and good corpses sounds odd if left with qualification. If they do have natures or functions, pebbles and corpses fully realize them and thus calling them "good" is redundant, or they have functions because of their relation to something that has a nature and aim for them, and thus calling them "good" is elliptical.
37 I am ignoring Williams' distinction between ethics and morality.
38 See Bernard Williams, *Morality: An Introduction to Ethics* (New York: Harper & Row, 1972); *Ethics and the Limits of Philosophy* (Cambridge: Harvard University Press, 1985).
39 Readers may be puzzled at my reconstruction of the *Gauguin Problem*. The puzzlement arises, because in the case of Gauguin there is a conflict between Gauguin realizing his artistic genius and realizing his familial responsibilities. Premise 2 is meant to be a generalization that includes cases like Gauguin's, but also cases where, rather than conflict arising between considerations of human nature and other considerations, there is simply independence.
40 Williams, *Morality*, 61.
41 A time-keeping device is a good one qua time-keeping device iff it tells time accurately. The various types of time-keeping devices will determine further standards of evaluation (e.g. watches need to tell time accurately and be lightweight, legible, etc.).
42 The lesson of the *Watch Problem* may help a bit (I stress *a bit*) with some interesting problems that arise in missiology (the study of missions). I know a number of native Africans who complain about the importation of Christianity. The main complaint (from both Christians and non-Christians) is that the importation of Christianity brought about a significant decline in African culture. The worry is that Christianity is incompatible with the diversity of cultures. The problem is not, it seems to me, with the complaint of the Africans. Rather, the problem is with the identification of Christianity with some specific culture. No doubt the importation of Christianity into a non-Christian area will result in the abandonment of certain beliefs and practices at odds with the beliefs and practices essential to Christianity. But this does not entail a total abandonment of the culture. For example, dress, language, dance, food, art, and other cultural features may largely remain intact after Christianity has become fixed, as it were. Thus, it is possible to have homogeneity at a basic level (fundamental beliefs, desires, etc.) and heterogeneity at non-basic levels.
43 Of course, this is precisely the worry that many come to after finishing Aristotle's *Nicomachean Ethics*. The contemplative life seems divorced from the political life. But the political life is where we find the "domesticated virtues" that Williams speaks of.

44 Thanks to Anselm Muller for this objection. According to Muller, the objection is due to Hare.
45 Geach, "Good and Evil," 69.
46 At the very least, the meaning of the term will include the correct category to which the referent belongs.
47 I am assuming that given the identity of nature and functions it is permissible to substitute one for the other *salva veritate*, at least in transparent contexts.
48 This does not imply that agreement about the nature and function of humans would settle every moral dispute. Many moral disputes have to do with the natures and functions of non-humans or the nature and function of various practices.
49 Thomson, "The Right and the Good," 296.
50 Ibid.
51 Ibid., 297.
52 Because Thomson's story and the story presented here are quite close on many details (see Chapter 2 for some of the details), attempting and failing to reconcile them will help us see exactly where the two stories differ.
53 Indeed, on at least one account of rationality, it is analytic that Thomson's ideal agent would have as a goal to be ideally rational.
54 Objection: The argument in the text begs the question. It presumes that rationality must be desired by everyone as an ideal goal. Reply: The argument in the text attempts to establish an inconsistency between Thomson's account and my account by assuming the correctness of my account. If my account is true, then Thomson's account is false. That is, since my account seems to imply that rationality must be desired as an ideal goal because of one's design function, and Thomson's account does not imply any such thing, the accounts are incompatible.
55 Thomson, "The Right and the Good," 293.
56 See Mark Bedau, "Where's the Good in Teleology?" *Philosophy and Phenomenological Research* 52 (1992): 781–801.

Chapter 4: The Function of "Good" and Good Functions

1 This way of breaking down the different accounts of functions is due to Michael Rea. See Michael Rea, *World Without Design: The Ontological Consequences of Naturalism* (Oxford: Oxford University Press, 2002), 108–27.
2 Rea, *World Without Design*, 114.
3 Of course, more needs to be said to defend this claim, but it is plausible. The best case for deriving ethics from such a meager base as survival and reproduction would seem to be one that attempts to show that

prisoner dilemma scenarios can yield the appropriate rules for cooperation. I am not confident that such attempts will deliver the goods.
4 Assuming, of course, that F and F^* are sufficiently different.
5 Rea, *World Without Design*, 116–17; Alvin Plantinga, *Warrant and Proper Function* (Oxford: Oxford University Press, 1993), 199–201.
6 Rea, *World Without Design*, 117.
7 Larry Wright's etiological account of functions is motivated in large part by examples like these. See Larry Wright, "Functions," *Philosophical Review* 82 (1973): 139–68.
8 Malfunction considerations provide much of the motivation behind Millikan's etiological account. See Ruth Millikan, *Language, Thought, and Other Biological Categories* (Cambridge: MIT Press, 1984); "In Defense of Proper Functions," *Philosophy of Science* 56 (1989): 288–302.
9 Quite obviously this objection relies on the claim that functions are relevant to evaluations. I am assuming that the arguments presented in Chapters 2 and 3 made the claim reasonable.
10 It may be countered that this first indirect objection simply assumes that SNF is false. If SNF were true, then a thing's goodness could still be determined by its function. I think this rebuttal misses the point. What the indirect objection elicits is further reason to regard SNF as susceptible to the direct objections. Someone unconvinced by the direct objections may become convinced after considering the first indirect objection.
11 Robert C. Koons presses these kinds of worries in his *Realism Regained: An Exact Theory of Causation, Teleology, and the Mind* (Oxford: Oxford University Press, 2000).
12 Rea makes this same point with respect to proper functions in *World Without Design*.
13 The case of artifacts is importantly different. Given the connection between natures and functions, the nature of an artifact is extrinsic because the function clearly is.
14 Ruth Millikan, *Language, Thought, and Other Biological Categories* (Cambridge: MIT Press, 1984).
15 Ibid., 17.
16 Ibid.
17 Millikan, "In Defense of Proper Functions," 288.
18 I realize that Millikan states that conditions (1) and (2) are *close to* sufficient. Nothing hangs on my stating her theory in terms of both necessary and sufficient conditions since both directions of the biconditional will be criticized.
19 Plantinga, *Warrant and Proper Function*, 203.
20 Rea, *World Without Design*, 120.
21 Plantinga, *Warrant and Proper Function*, 204.

22 Rea, *World Without Design*, 115.
23 Indeed, if EA and SNF purport to tell us the nature of functions, then it follows that there *could not* have been a first cell.
24 The defense of this premise is that cells are distinct from non-cells. Since distinctness implies necessary distinctness, cells have modal properties.
25 The defense of this premise is that the modal properties of a thing determine what the thing is and hence determine what it does or what it is supposed to do.
26 Both EA and SNF are committed to this premise.
27 Robert Koons, *Realism Regained: An Exact Theory of Causation, Teleology, and the Mind* (Oxford: Oxford University Press, 2000), 147–8.
28 Being a person, or perhaps being some other biological kind, may be a better example because Jesus Christ presents either a counterexample or the need for qualification. Being a human is not *the* most fundamental kind for Jesus, even though it is a fundamental kind for Him. Perhaps for Jesus we can say that his most fundamental kind is being both a human person and a divine person, but this appears to multiply persons in a way not congenial to orthodoxy. I can't pursue the matter further here, but suffice it to say that even if Jesus presents a counterexample to the general claim, it still seems likely that being a human is my most fundamental kind and that is all that is needed to get the argument going.
29 Objection: Does not God, in some sense, pass on the property of being human despite his not having the property of being human? Replies: First, in the case of God the act of bringing humans into being, whether this is an act of special creation or done through some other means, is quite different than what we are talking about here. God is the formal cause in the strict sense that He brings the form into being, whereas no creature is the formal cause of anything in that sense. Second, while God does not have (or is not) the property of being human, He does have all the perfections relevant for being human. Just as a regional manager may "pass on" the property of being a store supervisor even though the regional manager is not, strictly speaking a store supervisor, so too God can "pass on" being human, even though He is not human. Third, we can introduce a restricted quantifier here that explicitly excludes divine cases.
30 Earlier I raised some worries about the first member objection by noting that it seems to assume that first members cannot have F as a property without having F as a function. In this objection I am granting the assumption and attempting to raise a more difficult challenge.
31 Koons, *Realism Regained*, 147.
32 Plantinga, *Warrant and Proper Function*, 202.
33 While my focus will be on Robert C. Koons's account, Mark Bedau also argues for a normative account of function. See Mark Bedau, "Can

Biological Teleology be Naturalized," *The Journal of Philosophy* 88 (11) (1991): 647–55; "Where's the Good in Teleology?" *Philosophy and Phenomenological Research* 52 (1992): 781–801.
34 Koons, *Realism Regained*, 144.
35 Ibid., 145.
36 Note the connection between Koons's account and TMR. If something does not have a proper function, then it does not have a good. According to TMR, any expressions that the predicate-forming functor "good" takes as arguments must refer to things that have a nature and/or function.
37 Koons, *Realism Regained*, 146.
38 Ibid., 143.
39 Christopher Megone, "Aristotle's Function Argument and the Concept of Mental Illness," *Philosophy, Psychiatry, & Psychology* 5 (3) (1998): 195.
40 Rea, *World Without Design*, 122.
41 Ibid., 120.
42 Ibid. See also Bedau, "Can Biological Teleology be Naturalized."
43 Rea, *World Without Design*, 123.
44 Ibid., 124.
45 Indeed, Koons' account appears to imply that the only way to know that F is the proper function of x is to know what flourishing consists in for x.
46 Ibid., 113.
47 Ibid., 125.
48 There is a different diachronic case that I will not discuss because it is very similar to the first synchronic case I do discuss. According to the second diachronic reading of the objection, the artifact has a function that it can perform only after the self-destruct mechanism successfully performs its function. This implies that if the function of the artifact is distinct from the function of the self-destruct mechanism, then the artifact can never perform its function. I am not sure that in this case we have a genuine artifact.
49 I am assuming that it must be possible for the artifact to carry out its function in order for it to count as an artifact. If it is not possible for something to carry out its function, then it seems as though the thing is not an artifact.
50 I am assuming something like the thesis that intentions or desires are had or directed toward objects (or states of affairs) that the agent views as in some sense good for something. The "guise of the good" is a traditional doctrine and it has come under recent attack. See David Velleman, "The Guise of the Good," *Nous* 26 (1992): 3–26; Michael Stocker, "Desiring the Bad: an Essay in Moral Psychology," *Journal of Philosophy* 76 (1979): 738–53. For defenses of the "guise of the good" that respond to Velleman

and Stocker see Sergio Tenenbaum, *Appearances of the Good* (Cambridge: Cambridge University Press, 2007); Jennifer Hawkins, "Desiring the Bad Under the Guise of the Good," *The Philosophical Quarterly* 58 (231) (2007): 1–21; and Kieran Setiya, "Sympathy for the Devil," in *Desire, Practical Reason, and the Good*, ed. Sergio Tenenbaum (Oxford: Oxford university Press, 2010), 82–110. Setiya does not defend the traditional version of the guise of the good. He does make room for a weaker version of the guise of the good, according to which humans (as distinct from rational agents) normally intend or desire under the guise of the good. As far as I can tell, the weaker version is all that I need in order to adequately respond to the self-destruct objection.

51 Recall Chapter 2's discussion of Pigden's ICBM objection to the attributive account of "good."

52 This sentence and the last need some qualification, but such qualification would not render the point false though it would render the point more cumbersome.

53 It should be remembered that strictly speaking the claim is that the goodness of a thing is determined by its function *or* nature. But considering this objection to TMR is still instructive because TMR's ability to handle it shows the power of the normative account of functions coupled with the system/part distinction.

54 In fact, it is permissible to substitute in anything that has a nature, but the result will sound odd in some cases—for example, the pebble and corpse case (allowing that pebbles and corpses have natures)

Chapter 5: From the Attributive Account to God

1 Thomas Aquinas, *Summa Theologica* (1a, Q5, A1).

2 What about God? As we will see below, since it is plausible to regard God as transcending the normal categories of various kinds and substances, God is not a counterexample to this claim.

3 Admittedly there are some controversial metaphysical theses that I do not have the space to defend here, but that must be accepted in order for the alignment of the attributive account and the convertibility thesis to come together.

4 Aquinas, *Summa Theologica* (1a, Q48, A2). Quotation and translation from Herbert McCabe, *God and Evil in the Theology of St. Thomas Aquinas* (London: Continuum, 2010), 61–2.

5 I realize that it is odd to attribute the property of seeing to the human kind. But this is no more odd than attributing the property barking to the dog kind. Here, I take a decidedly Aristotelian stance on kind predication. For relevant discussion beyond the scope of this book see E. J. Lowe, *The Four-Category Ontology: A Metaphysical Foundation*

for Natural Science. (Oxford: Oxford University Press, 2006), and David Liebesman, "Simple Generics," *Nous* 45 (2011): 409–42.

6 In the tradition where PTE finds its most natural home, properties are typically those features of a substance that are intimately related to the substance's essence. The properties of a thing are necessary in the sense that they are features of a thing in every possible world in which the thing exists, but they are nevertheless not essential to the thing. In what follows I will be using properties in the modern sense of "any feature of a thing whatsoever."

7 Herbert McCabe, *God Matters* (London: Continuum, 2005), 29.

8 See Mark Larimore's "Evil as Privation: Seeing Darkness, Hearing Silence?" in *Deliver Us from Evil*, ed. M. David Eckel and Bradley L. Herling (London: Continuum, 2008), 149–68, for a particularly forceful and illuminating way of explication of this idea and bringing it to bear on some ethical issues.

9 Geach, "Good and Evil," 301.

10 "Is the Privation Theory of Evil Dead" *American Philosophical Quarterly* 44 (2007): 371–81.

11 See, for example, John F. Crosby, "Doubts about the Privation Theory that Will Not Go Away: Response to Patrick Lee," *American Catholic Philosophical Quarterly* 81 (2007): 489–505; Jorge J. E. Gracia, "Evil and the Transcendentality of Goodness: Suarez's Solution to the Problem of Positive Evils," in *Being and Goodness: The Concept of the Good in Metaphysics and Philosophical Theology*, ed. Scott MacDonald (New York: Cornell University Press, 1991).

12 In what follows I neither endorse nor reject the various theories of pain put forward. My primary aim here is simply to note that a number of accounts of pain (incompatible with each other) are compatible with PTE.

13 Murat Aydede, "Introduction: A Critical and Quasi-Historical Essay on Theories of Pain," in *Pain: New Essays on Its Nature and the Methodology of Its Study*, ed. Murat Aydede (Cambridge: MIT Press, 2005). Aydede does not endorse this view.

14 Michael Tye, "Another Look at Representationalism about Pain," in *Pain: New Essays on Its Nature and the Methodology of Its Study*, ed. Murat Aydede (Cambridge, MA: MIT Press, 2005), 100.

15 Ibid.

16 Todd Calder, "Is the Privation Theory of Evil Dead," *American Philosophical Quarterly* 44 (2007): 373.

17 Ibid.

18 Ibid, 106. Below we will consider some philosophical reasons for separating the sensory and affective components.

19 Tye, "Another Look at Representationalism about Pain," 112–13.

20 Ibid., 107.

21 Colin Klein, "An Imperative Theory of Pain," *Journal of Philosophy* 104 (2007): 520.
22 Ibid.
23 Ibid., 522.
24 Ibid., 526.
25 Aydede, "Introduction," 17.
26 Austen Clark, "Painfulness is not a Quale," in *Pain: New Essays on Its Nature and the Methodology of Its Study*, ed. Murat Aydede (Cambridge: MIT Press, 2005), 181.
27 Ibid., 184.
28 Mark Murphy, *An Essay on Divine Authority* (New York: Cornell University Press, 2002), 110.
29 Bill Anglin and Stewart Goetz, "Evil is Privation," *International Journal for Philosophy of Religion* 13 (1982): 3–12.
30 Calder, "Is the Privation Theory of Evil Dead," 374.
31 Ibid.
32 Ibid., 375.
33 My appeal to analogy will attempt to settle for an intuitive conception and will leave aside some of the logical niceties that inevitably arise. I think that this neglect will make the discussion easier to follow, and will not, in any event, be necessary to make sense of the claims made below.
34 In what follows I will focus on what is metaphysically the unifier of attributions of goodness, and not on the epistemology of such attributions. Thus, my account will appear to differ from that of Aquinas and other medievals who argue that applications of perfections to God are analogous. That is, it appears to them as though the focal meaning of the various perfections is something creaturely, not God. Ultimately, I think appearances are misleading here. What Aquinas and others are focusing on is the order of knowing. We come to know what the various perfections are by coming into contact with creatures. We then apply these perfections to God in an analogous way. But for Aquinas and others, God is the exemplar of the perfections. It is God who *is* the perfections, not the creature. See Ralph McInerny, "Saint Thomas on De hebdomadibus," in *Being and Goodness: The Concept of the Good in Metaphysics and Philosophical Theology*, ed. Scott MacDonald (New York: Cornell University Press, 1991), 74–97.
35 I owe the general idea for this argument to Alexander Pruss.
36 I am ignoring issues regarding the connection between conceivability and possibility.
37 This is similar to the argument Adams presents in *Finite and Infinite Goods* for the actual existence of the good itself. There are, however, significant differences between the two arguments. First, Adams's argument is explicitly Platonic in inspiration, while the one developed here is clearly Aristotelian. Second, and relatedly, Adams's argument and the

argument here have radically different starting points. Adams's argument begins by, in effect, denying the attributive account of "good" and focusing on the use of "good" that means excellent. Obviously, the argument presented here uses the attributive account as an initial premise. While the differences are significant, the arguments are similar in spirit.

38 See, for example, G. E. M. Anscombe and Peter T. Geach, *Three Philosophers: Aristotle, Aquinas, Frege* (Oxford: Blackwell, 1973), 71–128; Anthony Kenny, *The Five Ways: St. Thomas Aquinas' Proofs of God's Existence* (London: Routledge, 2008), 70–98; Christopher F. J. Martin, *Thomas Aquinas: God and Explanations* (Edinburgh: Edinburgh University Press, 1998), 171–8.

39 Aquinas, *Summa Theologica* (1a, Q2, A3).

40 Both are required, since the argument of this paragraph grants that cross-categorical comparison is problematic.

41 See Martin, *Thomas Aquinas: God and Explanations*, 177.

42 For more on how to reconcile the relational and intrinsic aspects of goodness see Jan A. Aersten, "Good as Transcendental and the Transcendence of the Good," in *Being and Goodness: The Concept of the Good in Metaphysics and Philosophical Theology*, ed. Scott MacDonald (New York: Cornell University Press, 1991).

43 See John Bigelow, Brian Ellis, and Caroline Lierse, "The World as One of a Kind: Natural Necessity and the Laws of Nature," *The British Journal for the Philosophy of Science* 43 (1992): 371–88.

44 See Stump's "Faith and the Problem of Evil," in *Seeking Understanding: The Stob Lectures, 1986–1998* (Grand Rapids, MI: William B. Eerdmans Publishing Company, 2001), and Adams's *Horrendous Evils and the Goodness of God* (Ithaca, NY: Cornell University Press, 1999).

45 No doubt there are many objections that could be raised against this line of thought. Perhaps the most pressing one comes from incommensurability issues. If there are goods and bads that are incommensurable with each other, then saying that there cannot be more evil than goodness *may* be false. A lot will depend on the exact content of the incommensurability, and issues regarding cross-categorical comparison will rear their heads here as well. I do not have much by way of a reply, since the objection can take many forms. But one thing to consider is that if incommensurability makes trouble for the claim that there cannot be more evil than goodness, it makes just as much trouble for the claim that there can be more evil than goodness. Thanks to Alexander Pruss for raising this concern.

46 Geach, "Good and Evil," 306.

Bibliography

Adams, Marilyn McCord. *Horrendous Evils and the Goodness of God*. Ithaca, NY: Cornell University Press, 1999.
Adams, Robert M. "Divine Command Metaethics Modified Again." *Journal of Religious Ethics* 7 (1979): 66–79.
—. *Finite and Infinite Goods: A Framework for Ethics*. Oxford: Oxford University Press, 1999.
Aersten, Jan A. "Good as Transcendental and the Transcendence of the Good." In *Being and Goodness: The Concept of the Good in Metaphysics and Philosophical Theology*, edited by Scott MacDonald, 56–73. New York: Cornell University Press, 1991.
Alter, Torin and Russell Daw. "Free Acts and Robot Cats." *Philosophical Studies* 102 (2001): 345–57.
Anglin, Bill and Stewart Goetz. "Evil is Privation." *International Journal for Philosophy of Religion* 13 (1982): 3–12.
Anscombe, G. E. M. and Peter T. Geach. *Three Philosophers: Aristotle, Aquinas, Frege*. Oxford: Blackwell, 1961.
Aydede, Murat. "Introduction: A Critical and Quasi-Historical Essay on Theories of Pain." In *Pain: New Essays on Its Nature and the Methodology of Its Study*, edited by Murat Aydede, 1–58. Cambridge: MIT Press, 2005.
Bealer, George. "The Philosophical Limits of Scientific Essentialism." *Philosophical Perspectives* 1 (1987): 289–365.
Bedau, Mark. "Can Biological Teleology be Naturalized." *The Journal of Philosophy* 88 (11) (1991): 647–55.
—. "Where's the Good in Teleology?" *Philosophy and Phenomenological Research* 52 (1992): 781–801.
Bigelow, John, Brian Ellis, and Caroline Lierse. "The World as One of a Kind: Natural Necessity and the Laws of Nature." *The British Journal for the Philosophy of Science* 43 (1992): 371–88.
Boyd, Richard. "How to Be a Moral Realist." In *Essays on Moral Realism*, edited by G. Sayre-McCord, 181–228. Ithaca: Cornell University Press, 1988.
Brink, David. "Moral Realism and the Skeptical Arguments from Disagreement and Queerness." *Australasian Journal of Philosophy* 62 (1984): 111–25.
—. "Externalist Moral Realism." *Southern Journal of Philosophy* Supplement (1986): 23–42.
—. *Moral Realism and the Foundations of Ethics*. Cambridge: Cambridge University Press, 1989.
Buller, David J. "Etiological Theories of Function: A Geographical Survey." *Biology and Philosophy* 13 (1998): 505–27.
Calder, Todd. "Is the Privation Theory of Evil Dead." *American Philosophical Quarterly* 44 (2007): 371–81.
Clark, Austen. "Painfulness is not a Quale." In *Pain: New Essays on Its Nature and the Methodology of Its Study*, edited by Murat Aydede, 177–98. Cambridge: MIT Press, 2005.

Copp, David. "Milk, Honey, and the Good Life on Moral Twin Earth." *Synthese* 124 (2000): 113–37.
—. "Introduction: Metaethics and Normative Ethics." In *The Oxford Handbook of Ethical Theory*, edited by David Copp, 3–35. Oxford: Oxford University Press, 2006.
—, ed. *Oxford Handbook of Ethical Theory*. Oxford: Oxford University Press, 2006.
Crosby, John F. "Doubts about the Privation Theory that will not go away: Response to Patrick Lee." *American Catholic Philosophical Quarterly* 81 (2007): 489–505.
Darwall, Stephen, Allan Gibbard, and Peter Railton. "Toward *fin de siecle* Ethics: Some Trends." *Philosophical Review* 101 (1992): 115–89.
Davies, Brian. *The Thought of Thomas Aquinas*. Oxford: Oxford University Press, 1993.
Devitt, Michael and Kim Sterelny. *Language and Reality*. 2nd edn. Cambridge: MIT Press, 1999.
Donnelly, John. "Some Remarks on Geach's Predicative and Attributive Adjectives." *Notre Dame Journal of Formal Logic* 12 (1) (1971): 125–8.
Fine, Kit. "Essence and Modality." *Philosophical Perspectives* 8 (1994): 1–16.
Foot, Philippa. *Natural Goodness*. Oxford: Oxford University Press, 2001.
Garcia, J. L. A. "Goods and Evils." *Philosophy and Phenomenological Research* 47 (3) (1987): 385–412.
Geach, Peter T. "Good and Evil." 1956. In *20th Century Ethical Theory*, edited by Steven M. Cahn and Joram G. Haber, 300–6. Upper Saddle River, NJ: Prentice Hall, 1995.
—. "Assertion." *Philosophical Review* 74 (1965): 449–65.
—. "A Program for Syntax." *Synthese* 22 (1970): 3–17.
—. *The Virtues*. Cambridge: Cambridge University Press, 1977.
Gertzler, Jyl. "The Attractions and Delights of Goodness." *The Philosophical Quarterly* 54 (216) (2004): 353–67.
Gracia, Jorge J. E. "Evil and the Transcendentality of Goodness: Suarez's Solution to the Problem of Positive Evils." In *Being and Goodness: The Concept of the Good in Metaphysics and Philosophical Theology*, edited by Scott MacDonald, 151–76. New York: Cornell University Press, 1991.
Gray, Richard. "Natural Phenomenon Terms." *Analysis* 66 (2) (2006): 141–8.
Griffin, James. *Well-Being: Its Meaning, Measurement, and Moral Importance*. Oxford: Clarendon Press, 1986.
Hampshire, Stuart. "Ethics: A Defense of Aristotle." In *Freedom of Mind and Other Essays*. Princeton: Princeton University Press, 1971.
Hare, R. M. *The Language of Morals*. Oxford: Oxford University Press, 1952.
—. "Geach: Good and Evil." *Analysis* 18 (1957) 103–12.
Hawkins, Jennifer. "Desiring the Bad Under the Guise of the Good." *The Philosophical Quarterly* 58 (2007): 1–21.
Horgan, Terence and Mark Timmons. "New Wave Moral Realism Meets Moral Twin Earth." *Journal of Philosophical Research* 16 (1990–91): 447–65.
—. "Troubles for New Wave Moral Semantics: The 'Open Question Argument' Revived." *Philosophical Papers* 21 (1992): 153–75.
—. "Troubles on Moral Twin Earth: Moral Queerness Revived." *Synthese* 92 (1992): 221–60.
—. "From Moral Realism to Moral Relativism in One Easy Step." *Critica* 28 (1996): 3–39.
—. "Copping Out on Moral Twin Earth." *Synthese* 124 (2000): 139–52.

—. "Analytical Moral Functionalism Meets Moral Twin Earth." In *Minds, Ethics, and Conditionals: Themes from the Philosophy of Frank Jackson*, edited by Ian Ravenscroft, Oxford: Oxford University Press, 2009.

Hursthouse, Rosalind. *On Virtue Ethics*. Oxford: Oxford University Press, 1999.

Kenny, Anthony. *The Five Ways: St. Thomas Aquinas' Proofs of God's Existence*. London: Routledge, 1969.

Klein, Colin. "An Imperative Theory of Pain." *Journal of Philosophy* 104 (2007): 517–32.

Koons, Robert C. *Realism Regained: An Exact Theory of Causation, Teleology, and the Mind*. Oxford: Oxford University Press, 2000.

Korsgaard, Christine M. *The Sources of Normativity*. Cambridge: Cambridge University Press, 1996.

Kripke, Saul. *Naming and Necessity*. Cambridge: Harvard University Press, 1980

—. "Identity and Necessity." 1971. In *Metaphysics: The Big Questions*, edited by Peter van Inwagen and Dean W. Zimmerman, 519–43. Malden: Blackwell Publishing, 2008.

Lahav, Ran. "Against Compositionality: The Case of Adjectives." *Philosophical Studies* 57 (3) (1989): 261–79.

Larimore, Mark. "Evil as Privation: Seeing Darkness, Hearing Silence?" In *Deliver Us from Evil*, edited by M. David Eckel and Bradley L. Herling, 149–68. London: Continuum, 2008.

Laurence, Stehpen and Eric Margolis, eds. *Creations of the Mind: Essays on Artifacts and their Representation*. Oxford: Oxford University Press, 2007.

Lewis, David. *Parts of Classes*. Oxford: Basil Blackwell, 1991.

Liebesman, David. "Simple Generics." *Nous* 45 (2011): 409–42.

Loux, Michael. "Toward an Aristotelian Theory of Abstract Objects." In *Midwest Studies in Philosophy: Studies in Essentialism* 11, edited by Peter French, Theodore Uehling, and Howard Wettstein, 495–512. Minneapolis, MN: University of Minnesota Press, 1986.

Lowe, E. J. *The Four-Category Ontology: A Metaphysical Foundation for Natural Science*. Oxford: Oxford University Press, 2006.

MacDonald, Scott, ed. *Being and Goodness: The Concept of the Good in Metaphysics and Philosophical Theology*. New York: Cornell University Press, 1991.

MacKay, Alfred F. "Attributive-Predicative." *Analysis* 30 (1970): 113–20.

Martin, Christopher F. J. *Thomas Aquinas: God and Explanations*. Edinburgh: Edinburgh University Press, 1998.

McCabe, Herbert. *God Matters*. London: Continuum, 2005.

—. *God and Evil in the Theology of St. Thomas Aquinas*. London: Continuum, 2010.

McInerny, Ralph. "Saint Thomas on De hebdomadibus." In *Being and Goodness: The Concept of the Good in Metaphysics and Philosophical Theology*, edited by Scott MacDonald, 74–97. New York: Cornell University Press, 1991.

—. *Aquinas on Human Action: A Theory of Practice*. Washington, DC: Catholic University of America Press, 1992.

Megone, Christopher. "Aristotle's Function Argument and the Concept of Mental Illness." *Philosophy, Psychiatry, & Psychology* 5 (3) (1998): 187–201.

Merricks, Trenton. *Objects and Persons*. Oxford: Clarendon Press, 2001.

Miller, Richard. "A Purely Causal Solution to One of the Qua-Problems for the Causal Theory of Reference." *Australasian Journal of Philosophy* 70 (4) (1992): 425–34.

Millikan, Ruth. *Language, Thought, and Other Biological Categories*. Cambridge: MIT Press, 1984.

—. "In Defense of Proper Functions." *Philosophy of Science* 56 (1989): 288–302.

Moore, G. E. *Principia Ethica*. rev. edn, edited by Thomas Baldwin. Cambridge: Cambridge University Press, 1993.

Murphy, Mark. *An Essay on Divine Authority*. New York: Cornell University Press, 2002.

Paul, L. A. "In Defense of Essentialism." *Philosophical Perspectives* 20 (2006): 333–72.

Pigden, Charles. "Geach on Good." *The Philosophical Quarterly* 40 (159) (1990): 129–54.

Plantinga, Alvin. *The Nature of Necessity*. Oxford: Clarendon Press, 1974.

—. *Warrant and Proper Function*. Oxford: Oxford University Press, 1993.

Porter, Jean. *Nature as Reason: A Thomistic Theory of the Natural Law*. Grand Rapids, MI: Erdmans, 2005.

Portner, Paul H. *What is Meaning?: Fundamentals of Formal Semantics*. Oxford: Blackwell, 2005.

Putnam, Hilary. "The Meaning of 'Meaning'." In *Mind, Language and Reality, Philosophical Papers*, 215–71. Cambridge: Cambridge University Press, 1975.

Rea, Michael. "In Defense of Mereological Universalism." *Philosophy and Phenomenological Research* 58 (2) (1998): 347–60.

—. *World Without Design: The Ontological Consequences of Naturalism*. Oxford: Oxford University Press, 2002.

Rudder-Baker, Lynne. "The Ontology of Artifacts." *Philosophical Explorations* 7 (2) (2004): 99–111.

—. "On the Twofold Nature of Artefacts." *Studies in History and Philosophy of Science* 37 (2006): 132–6.

Sainsbury, Mark. *Logical Forms: An Introduction to Philosophical Logic*. Oxford: Blackwell, 1991.

Salmon, Nathan. *Reference and Essence*. Princeton, NJ: Princeton University Press, 1981.

Sayre-McCord, Geoffrey, ed. *Essays on Moral Realism*. Ithaca, NY: Cornell University Press, 1988.

—. "Moral Realism." In *The Oxford Handbook of Ethical Theory*, edited by David Copp, 39–62. Oxford: Oxford University Press, 2006.

Setiya, Kieran. "Sympathy for the Devil." In *Desire, Practical Reason, and the Good*, edited by Sergio Tenenbaum, 82–110. Oxford: Oxford University Press, 2010.

Shafer-Landau, Russ. *Moral Realism: A Defense*. Oxford: Oxford University Press, 2003

Simpson, Robert W. "Good and Bad." *Canadian Journal of Philosophy* 12 (1) (1982): 101–17.

Soames, Scott. "Kripke on Epistemic and Metaphysical Possibility: Two Routes to the Necessary Aposteriori." In *Saul Kripke*, edited by Alan Berger, 78–99. Cambridge: Cambridge University Press, 2011.

Stalnaker, Robert. "Reference and Necessity." In *Blackwell Companions to Philosophy: A Companion to the Philosophy of Language*, edited by Bob Hale and Crispin Wright. Oxford: Wiley-Blackwell, 1999.

Stevenson, John G. "Donnelly on Geach." *Notre Dame Journal of Formal Logic* 13 (3) (1972): 429–30.

Stocker, Michael. "Desiring the Bad: an Essay in Moral Psychology." *Journal of Philosophy* 76 (1979): 738–53.

Stump, Eleonore. "Faith and the Problem of Evil." In *Seeking Understanding: The Stob Lectures, 1986–1998*, 491–550. Grand Rapids, MI: William B. Eerdmans Publishing Company, 2001.

Szabo, Zoltan Gendler. "Adjectives in Context." In *Perspectives on Semantics, Pragmatics, and Discourse*, edited by Istvan Kenesei and Robert M. Harnish, 119–45. Amsterdam: John Benjamins Publishing Company, 2001.

Tenenbaum, Sergio. *Appearances of the Good*. Cambridge: Cambridge University Press, 2007.

Thomson, Judith J. "On Some Ways in Which a Thing Can be Good." *Social Philosophy and Policy* 9 (2) (1992): 96–117.

—. "The Right and the Good." *The Journal of Philosophy* 94 (2) (1997): 273–98.

—. *Goodness and Advice*. Princeton: Princeton University Press, 2001.

—. "The Legacy of Principia." *Southern Journal of Philosophy* 41 Supplement (2003): 62–83.

—. *Normativity*. Peru: Open Court, 2008.

Tye, Michael. "Mental States, Adverbial Theory of." In *Routledge Encyclopedia of Philosophy*, edited by E. Craig. London: Routledge, 1998.

—. "Another Look at Representationalism about Pain." In *Pain: New Essays on Its Nature and the Methodology of Its Study*, edited by Murat Aydede, 99–120. Cambridge: MIT Press, 2005.

van Inwagen, Peter. *Material Beings*. Ithaca, NY: Cornell University Press, 1990.

van Inwagen, Peter and Dean W. Zimmerman, eds. *Metaphysics: The Big Questions*. Malden: Blackwell Publishing, 2008.

Velleman, David. "The Guise of the Good." *Nous* 26 (1992): 3–26.

Vendler, Zeno. *Linguistics in Philosophy*. Ithaca, NY: Cornell University Press, 1967.

von Wright, George Henrik. *The Varieties of Goodness*. London: Routledge, 1964.

Walsh, Denis. "Evolutionary Essentialism." *British Journal for the Philosophy of Science* 57 (2006): 425–48.

Williams, Bernard. *Morality: An Introduction to Ethics*. New York: Harper & Row, 1972.

—. *Ethics and the Limits of Philosophy*. Cambridge: Harvard University Press, 1985.

Wright, Larry. "Functions." *Philosophical Review* 82 (1973): 139–68.

Zagzebski, Linda. *Divine Motivation Theory*. Cambridge: Cambridge University Press, 2004.

Zimmerman, Michael. "In Defense of the Concept of Intrinsic Value." *Canadian Journal of Philosophy* 29 (1999): 389–410.

—. *The Nature of Intrinsic Value*. Lanham: Rowman & Littlefield Publishers, Inc., 2001.

Index

a posteriori 2, 7, 15–16, 18–20, 24–9, 49–54, 56
  moral naturalism 9, 17, 30
  moral supernaturalism 17, 30
  necessity 1, 19, 22, 24, 26–7, 29–30, 52, 54, 56
a priori 8, 10, 12, 15–16, 18–20, 25–8, 49, 52–3
  necessary 18–19
Adams, Marilyn McCord 121
Adams, Robert M. 1, 6, 18–30
adjunctive 41, 46, 60
  adjunct 41–2, 47
adverbial 54–5
  adverbialism 54–5
alienans 32–3, 36–8, 98, 100
analogous 20, 23, 27, 68, 84, 111–13, 115–16, 119
  analogical 111–12
  analogy 54–5, 96, 106, 111, 114–15, 117, 119
analytic 7–10, 16, 27–8, 31, 53
  moral naturalism 9, 14, 17, 30
  moral supernaturalism 10, 30
Anglin, Bill 109
artifact 39–40, 43–4, 58–9, 62, 66–7, 69, 76, 79, 84–8
attributive 1–2, 4–5, 30–3, 35–8, 40–1, 43, 46–57, 59–63, 88, 90–1, 93, 95–100, 102–3, 110–11, 113–23
Aydede, Murat 101

Boyd, Richard 1, 6, 10–12, 14, 30
Buller, David J. 3

Calder, Todd 101, 103, 108–9
categories 71, 75, 96, 112–13, 116–20

causal theory of reference (CTR) 11–13, 20, 23–4, 66
  hybrid causal theory of reference (HCTR) 13–14, 16
Clark, Austen 107
comparative 51
convertibility of being and goodness 4, 90–2, 96, 114, 118, 121–2
  convertibility thesis 4, 91, 93–5, 98–101, 119, 122–3
Copp, David 7–8
corpse 59–61

descriptivism 10, 16, 23

empirical 11, 15–18, 20, 24–9, 52–3
  empirically 12, 26, 28, 50, 53–4
equivocal 111
essence 3, 16, 34–5, 41, 47, 50, 53–4, 57–8, 62, 99
essentialism,
  Aristotelian 3
evolution 3, 70
  evolutionary theory 3–4, 71, 75, 80
  natural selection 3, 44, 78

Fine, Kit 57–8, 62–3
focal meaning 111–13, 119
Foot, Philippa 2
fourth way 114–16, 118
function 2–3, 23, 32, 34–6, 38, 40–1, 43–7, 49–50, 56–64, 66–90, 93, 97, 100, 102, 107, 111, 119–21
  etiological 2, 70–2, 74–6, 78–80
  normative 2, 71–2, 80, 82–3, 86–9, 121
  statistical 2, 71–2

gauguin problem 63–4
Geach, Peter T. 1–2, 4–5, 30–8, 40–1, 43–8, 60, 66–7, 98, 100, 124
Gertzler, Jyl 60
Goetz, Stewart 109

Hare, R. M. 2, 66–8
Hursthouse, Rosalind 2

ideal goal 43–5, 68–70
imperative,
  content 105–6
  sensations 105–6
  theory of pain 105, 107
intension,
  intensionality 50
intention 39–40, 42, 51, 55, 87–8, 109–10, 114
  first-order 47
  meta-level 88
intersective 33

kind 4, 10–13, 15, 23–4, 29, 33–6, 38–40, 43, 46–7, 50–1, 53, 56–9, 61–3, 65–6, 71–5, 77–83, 85, 87, 90, 92–4, 97, 99–105, 110–12, 115–24
  human 39, 63, 65, 123
  natural 10, 12–13, 16–17, 19–21, 59, 66
  natural kind term 10–11, 13, 16–17, 20–4, 26, 66
  primary 57–8, 65, 89, 95
Klein, Colin 105–6
Koons, Robert C. 2, 78, 80–5, 121
Kripke, Saul 7–8, 10–11, 23, 31, 52–3
Kripkean 6

Loux, Michael 55–6

McCabe, Herbert 99
MacKay, Alfred 36–7
Megone, Christopher 83
metaethics 4–5, 19–20, 35, 111, 120
  metaethical 2–6, 22, 27, 48–9, 91

Millikan, Ruth 74–6
Moore, G. E. 2, 6, 8–10, 17, 29, 36, 41, 43
moral disagreement 1, 67–8, 127–8
moral realism 1–2, 6–11, 17–18, 29–31, 55, 67–8, 71–2, 88
  naturalistic 6, 9, 14, 17
  Platonic 18
  Platonism 18–20
  realist 6–10, 17, 56
  supernaturalistic 6, 18
  teleological (TMR) 2–4, 71–2, 80, 88–90, 113
  theistic 18–20, 25
moral supernaturalism 6, 10, 17–18, 29–30
moral terms 11–13, 23
multiple realizability 16
  multiply realizable 16
Murphy, Mark 108

natural 3, 10, 16, 60, 76, 119
  property 8, 10–12, 14, 49
naturalism 11, 14
  ethical 2
  moral 6, 9–10, 14, 17, 30
natures 3–4, 16, 21, 34, 41, 46, 48–9, 54, 57–63, 66–7, 74, 82, 88, 111, 119–20
news 61
non-intersective 33

ontological argument 22, 27, 113, 116
open question argument (OQA) 6, 8–12, 14–17, 29–30, 49

pain 4, 55, 100–8
painasymbolia syndrome 107
pebble 59–61
Pigden, Charles 37–40, 46
Plantinga, Alvin 73, 76–7, 80–1
Porter, Jean 3, 4
predicate-forming functor 5, 41, 50, 56, 90, 93
predicative 31–3, 35–6, 38, 41, 47

Index

privation theory of evil (PTE) 4, 91, 95–100, 103–5, 107–9, 114, 122–4
problem of evil 4, 91, 120–2
proper names 6, 13
property marker 5, 90, 93, 95, 111, 115
Putnam, Hilary 7, 10, 23, 31
Putnamian 6

qua problem 13, 15, 17, 23, 66–7
 moral qua problem 13, 17

rational animal 58, 63, 69
Rea, Michael 58, 73, 76–7, 83–5, 87–8
representationalism 104–5
 representational 104–5, 107
 representationalist 102, 104–5
 strong 105
rigid designator 6, 11
 rigidity 11

Sayre-McCord, Geoffrey 8–9
semantic relativism 110–11, 117–18

semantics 2, 10–11, 18–21, 23, 25–6, 30, 46–7, 52, 54
Soames, Scott 53
Socratic 60
Stalnaker, Robert 23
Stump, Eleonore 121
substantive 8, 35–6, 43, 45–8, 60, 65, 100
sunset 61–2, 89–90, 121
supernatural 10
 property 8, 49
synthetic 7, 9–10, 12, 14, 16–17, 28, 31, 51, 54, 56–7
 a posteriori 7

teleological 3
Thomson, Judith J. 5, 41–7, 59–60, 68–71
Tye, Michael 55, 101–2, 104

univocal 111, 116

Walsh, Denis 3, 4
Williams, Bernard 63–5

Zimmerman, Michael 47–8

Made in the USA
San Bernardino, CA
20 August 2015